KAT KERR

Foreword by Scribe Angels (expounded)

REVEALING HEAVEN

II

An Eyewitness Account continued

ILLUSTRATED BY

WALTER REYNOLDS

Printed in the United States of America

ISBN 9781609578633

Illustrated by Walter Reynolds

Cover design by Tim Dahn

Cover photograph and author photo by Jennifer Voorhees/Clicks by JVO

Cover illustration by Walter Reynolds

www.xulonpress.com

➤┤◆➤━◯━◄┤━◄

HEAVEN

By Kat Kerr

Oh, how fair is that wondrous place, where finally you see Him face to face,

What passion you find in those beautiful eyes; so much it causes your heart all evil to despise.

Many times angels kept me from hands of death, they came so near, I felt Heaven's breath,

My life one day will tell hope's story, the days of being hidden in unspeakable Glory,

Forever grateful to have lived surrendered every hour, and that I had been willing in the day of His Power,

In the fullness of time, the Spirit will catch me up, no more to roam; place me in the Fathers arms, I am home!

ENDORSEMENTS

>─┤◆├─◉─┤◆├─<

Kat Kerr is a true example of carrying the power of God. Her life is undoubtedly one that the Father can use and the testimony of the reality of Heaven is one that needs to be shared with all. The Holy Spirit has brought this book into our lives for this time in Eternity. Unlike many other books written about Heaven, this book actually shows you picturesque images of our Heavenly home. How neat is that? It truly brings Heaven to life because it is LIFE changing. After reading this book you will never be the same nor would you want to be! Please do not miss reading Revealing Heaven II.

La'Faye M. Jones
Atlanta, Georgia

To be able to speak on the character of my sister is an honor; she truly has the mind of God. She is lifting a standard of holiness, while revealing Heaven to God's people. When God revealed to Kat about the Stones of Fire, I was in awe of Him because of my love and work with gemstones. I looked up sapphires in my gemologist book and it says that in ancient times, people believed this gem represented royalty and that you would receive blessings from Heaven. I now know everything beautiful comes from the heart of God, even gemstones! My advice to everyone would be to read Kat's series on Revealing Heaven.

Tamekka Hayes
Gemologist & Jeweler
San Diego, CA

After reading Kat's first book it gave us such joy learning about what Heaven is really like. Our family was so blessed to get to know Kat when we hosted her meetings; she is truly the real deal. You can feel the love of God radiating out of her, she has such a compassion for people and even made time to speak in the prison. Reading the second book will give you more revelation of who God is and the beautiful illustrations will give you a look into what God has waiting for His people in Heaven.

The Abbey Family
Montville, Ohio

Kat Kerr is a real woman of God with NOW time revelation of Heaven. As someone who has visited Heaven, the words she writes are true and real. As a parent of a child that has transitioned ahead of me to Heaven, Kat's first and now this book has brought comfort and confirmation of things I have seen myself. Kat's revelations of places like the Stones of Fire within the Father, set my soul aflame and yearning for more! Revealing Heaven II is a must read to those who desire to drink deep of the Father.

Ki Michael, Intercessor
Jacksonville, FL

ACKNOWLEDGEMENT FOR DOOR OPENERS

>―‹›―○―‹›―‹

Please accept my eternal gratitude for your continued
contributions to further the Revelation of
Heaven

Ms. Lafaye Jones, GA

Pastors Tony & Cynthia Brazelton, VCMI, MD,
DC, VA

Sister Billye Brim, Prayer Mountain, MO

Pastor Thomas & Annie Mae Warren, New
Freedom, MS

Mrs. Brenda King, FL

Mrs. Nadine Young, Activation Ministries, CO

The Abbe Family, OH

Becky Brock and Vicki & Mike Tolbert, OK

Liska Henderson and Victoria & Ron Wilson, CA

THANK YOU
(Sincerely grateful)

To my Dad, for raising me in Holiness, showing me how to love others and always see the 'good' in people. I believe he knew all along, that I would turn out just fine! P.S. Loved the donuts and Chocolate milk!

To my Mom, for loving me, even when I was high maintenance as a kid and for assuring me that I was 'strange' almost every day of my life while growing up. Also, for all the times she paid me with candy bars for babysitting my multitude of siblings (I earned every delicious bite)!

To my beautiful daughters, Kelly, Kimberly & Kasey for not running away and changing their identity when I (with pink hair) announced to the world that I made regular trips to Heaven and would be teaching everyone a dance the angels do; knowing full well I had been thrown out of a jazzercise class!

To my husband the Captain, for loving and protecting me for 33 years; thank God he called me a 'keeper' and not a 'catch & release'!

To my brothers and sisters for sharpening me to a fine point, while growing up with them. We made a great team and it prepared me for life!

To Margaret, who shall receive a great reward for pouring her life into One Quest, even when it took over her home! It was worth it all wasn't it, even when we had to do the Angel Dance in the car at 3:00 am to stay awake while driving to a speaking engagement.

To Jen, for obeying God when He said He was giving her to me for a season, even though she cried in the beginning. The only thing that really helped was the fact that I had pink hair and I let her have blue at the same time! Great job on Facebook Jen!

To RJ, for the thousands of CDs and DVDs he burned, labeled and mailed out with almost no pay, except occasional chocolate chip cookies and a few dollars for bidding on eBay!

To Alice (my BFF while growing up), for all your encouragement and support (both financial & prayers) even when you may not have agreed with everything I said; you loved me!

To Patricia, who never gave up on me, defended me even though I didn't need it and blessed me personally.

To the Father, for revealing His heart to me and for trusting me with this holy assignment to reveal Heaven to earth.

To my beloved Jesus, for sharing eternity with me; asking me to put pink highlights in my hair and visiting me often to encourage me.

To Holy Spirit, my best friend, who invaded my life continually, caught me up to tour Heaven; and for all the times He made me laugh.

To all those men and women of God who Hosted our One Quest Team to come and share Heaven.

To all those who embraced God's revelation of Heaven and allowed it to change their lives and then shared it with others!

AUTHOR'S NOTE

>∺+⟨>⟨⊙⟩⟨>+⟨∺

Please be sure to read Volume I of Revealing Heaven if you have not done so. It is an introduction to the revelations I received in Heaven and necessary to fully comprehend the deeper revelations in Volume II. Volume I opened your understanding to the fact that Heaven is a literal place where you actually LIVE an amazing life after departing! Thousands of lives were impacted as they were taken 'out of the box' and given the truth about the life in Heaven you enjoy while living in the presence of an awesome, loving God!

In Volume II, you will receive more revelation about places in Heaven, how Heaven operates here on earth and what our relationships will be like in Heaven. God also reveals some of the greatest mysteries that have been hidden in the Word since the world began!

One of the most profound revelations the Father gives in this book is the fast approaching, greatest move of God the earth will ever experience, Joel 2, the Great Awakening; when He will pour out His spirit on ALL flesh! Nothing will remain the same as it empowers every Believer with His love and they carry His Glory around the earth.

God will entrust His secrets to His friends, those who have surrendered everything and those who are not afraid to live a Supernatural life. You cannot be afraid of the face of man, if you are to boldly proclaim what God has said or what He has shown you! If you are grounded in the Word and He rules from the throne of your heart, you will hear His voice. All these things have been required of me, to 'lose' my life so that the Truth can be revealed from a pure heart and clean hands. There can be no agenda of my own, only His ways and His will in my life! There are many things in my life He asked me to give up and I did it gladly to have the relationship I have with Him!

Let me say that the things of God are not discerned by the flesh (your natural mind), but through your spirit with the help of the Holy Spirit. Good reading and I pray it will change forever your view of eternity and widen your understanding that the Father is UNLIMITED in His ability to create and in His desire to love you. Get ready to have the deeper things revealed as God is taking us to a higher level, so come up and see!

FOREWORD

(A prophetic Proclamation from God)

By
The Scribe Angels

To Him who sits upon the throne, we give Praise, Honor and Glory forever and ever, that He would desire to reveal His home in the Heavens to the men of Earth. **Rejoice, O Earth, Rejoice!** For Heaven is about to kiss you and when it does, the Fire of His Passion will consume every living being. He will forever leave His mark on the hearts of millions and they shall come to know Him as their Savior. Be thankful citizens of Earth that you are living in this day and hour, when the Glory of the Lord will cover the whole Earth. How magnificent in His ways, how mighty in His acts is the hand of Him who sits upon the throne. In eternity they shall sing about these days- the great and powerful days before the end comes. All things will be shaken and all things will be restored to and through God's faithful believers!

Prepare O enemies of the Most High, to be made His footstool! None will escape His Glory and there will be no place to hide from His Light! He who has chosen this handmaiden to reveal the hidden things, the precious things, and the treasures stored up in His Heaven for those who love Him and love the coming of Him! We, His faithful Scribes, created by Him in the beginning to serve in His celestial realm and to record the words of those we are sent for; and to deliver and release His messages to those whom He trusts- are grateful to be a part of His divine plan in revealing Heaven.

Prepare you faithful ones, whom have stood under much warfare and devastation of the enemy. Prepare to receive great reward, now, in this lifetime and in the glorious life to come. You are about to see the power of your God released, and you will truly know He is in control.

Behold, His fire comes to blaze across this world and into the hearts of men, to push back the great darkness and claim His creation back to Himself.

Prepare men and women of God, those who watch over the souls of their congregations- to yield to the Holy Spirit of God when asked to lay down your plans, man's plans, and allow Him to take control during this hour. For those who yield, there shall be great increase of anointing in your ministry. For those who refuse to yield, your place shall be given to another and some will even sleep early! **Prepare your hearts,** for He must first visit His leaders and then His church body. **Will you all be able to stand and carry this Glory, or will you be exposed by its coming?**

The bowls before the altar are tipping and the veil of flesh has been torn; nothing or no one can stop what is about to happen! Manifestations of His power through signs, wonders and the miraculous will happen everywhere- no building will be able to contain them. **He will no longer be put in a box, nor wear man's tag,** but He will unite His true Body of believers and the World will know them by their love for each other! Prepare to hear a new sound- the sound of Heaven!

This is a glimpse into Eternity! Prepare to read. Prepare to be forever changed. Prepare people of Earth for God is *REVEALING HEAVEN!*

AMEN! AMEN! AMEN!

EXPOUNDING ON FOREWORD

Even though this Foreword was the same one given in Volume I, the Father requested it be repeated in Volumes II and III due to the importance of it. His will is to make sure everyone who reads the series on the revelations of Heaven, understands what He is about to do on this earth. It will alert people to get their lives in order and prepare to carry His Glory and do the greater works that Christ talked about.

When His Spirit is poured out on all flesh (Joel 2) and God's people start operating like Him, the 'gray' area (that says there is no God) will be erased and there will be no more excuses to prevent people from making a decision. The knowledge of the Glory of the Lord will cover the earth as the waters cover the sea; it will touch every living human being! This will also be a warning to all who are enemies of God that they will not be able to escape the testimony of His power in His people and ALL will have to make a choice to either remain a part of the great darkness or chose Christ, the Greater Glory.

The Lord asked me to tell His people, "The next 15 years will be the most exciting time to be alive on this earth as a Believer"! *There will be manifestations of miracles and signs & wonders that have never* *been seen before. Heaven has also declared that they are going to EMPTY the body parts warehouse during the greatest healing revival ever! So stand up and declare what God meant when He said, "Let us make man in our image and after our likeness". This meant their outside image (flesh) and also their inside image (spirit). The Word says we are the temple of the Holy Spirit and the fullness of the Godhead bodily; so we need to start living like we believe it! During this outpouring, God will also bless His people (who have been faithful) financially and they will be able to carry out the vision He gave them (even if it was years ago).*

Allow the Holy Spirit to reveal anything in your life that is hindering you in your relationship with God. Also, start speaking life with your words and not negative, fear filled words (study the book of James). Repent and speak over your family, what Heaven says: They will become 'mighty men and women of God', they 'will NOT miss their destiny' and that they will become a 'living testimony of the saving power of Jesus Christ'. Do not declare what they are doing in darkness, call them into the Kingdom of Light; that way you release faith for their salvation. Philippians says our citizenship is in Heaven, so let us start acting like it and declare: Your will be done in earth (in our lives) as it is in Heaven! According to the

Word, nothing of the enemy exists there; Witchcraft is NOT in Heaven, Vampires are NOT in Heaven, and abortion is NOT in Heaven; so should we be inviting those things in our lives by watching, reading or agreeing with them? The Holy Spirit said tell everyone, "Whatever you enter into, will enter into you"; that means we need to guard our hearts, minds and spirits by making the right choices.

God wants His people to live victorious now, not just when they get to Heaven. If you truly want to be used by Him for something great, then you must lay down your own rights, opinions and agendas and take His! Do not withhold God from intervening in your life by living by the world's standards, live by His! Be a part of the greatest move of God this world will ever see because it WILL happen with or without you! PURSUE HIM!!!

INTRODUCTION

Those who love Him have cried out for revelation on the mysteries of Heaven and God is now answering those cries! Because He has chosen this time in eternity to reveal himself and His home, I have been caught up to Heaven, like John in book of Revelations, for the purpose of sharing it with others. I pray your eyes and ears are opened, that you may hear what God has sent from His Storehouse of Revelation. This book will usher in knowledge of the Greater Glory instead of the great darkness that now covers our earth! Make room in your heart for these profound revelations of the Holy One and His home, Heaven! It will cause the fear of death to be swallowed up and let your mind begin to dwell in heavenly places with the Lord as you read Revealing Heaven II.

These revelations can only be spiritually discerned, so if you struggle with them; you need to spend more time in His presence and read them again. It is not for my benefit that they were revealed to me, but for you and every one who desires a greater understanding of who the Godhead is and what they have prepared for those that love them! They want you to KNOW them, because they love you. The Father made you; Christ (Messiah) died for you and Holy Spirit guides you because they want a family to spend eternity with! The only key that will open that door of eternal life is salvation through the blood of Christ; there is no other way!

Revealing Heaven II takes you deeper into the things of God and the place called "Heaven". In order to fully comprehend this book, you need to read volume I, which is an introduction to the heavenly realm and the understanding of how great God is. You will NEVER think of God, Heaven or yourself the same way again. You will LIVE with an expectancy you never had before. As we enter into a HOLY season of Heaven being poured out on this earth so we might do the greater works, you need to prepare yourself and your family to do more than just watch it come; you need to be ready to MAKE it happen! If you are serious about being a part of the Great Awakening (Joel 2) then you will surrender (everything) as I have. It will be worth everything, to gain Him (life itself).

I have prayed diligently for all those who read these words poured out from the Father's heart. Because He taught me well, I forgive any who speak against me or against this work which He commissioned. Please, Father do not hear their harsh words or accusations and I ask that you not even write them down or charge it to their account. Forgive them, and loose the Holy Spirit to pursue them that they might know you and be free! Blessings to all who seek Him and find Him!

TABLE OF CONTENTS

➤—◆—◯—◆—◄

The Lord God will do nothing but He revealed
His secrets to His friends the Prophets first!
Amos 3:7 (KJV)

(Permission granted from Father Heart Communications)

CHAPTER ONE

The Ways of Heaven

❧⟡❧

This book will take you on a journey that will surpass anything you have ever experienced, so make sure you read it with no distractions. It captivates and catches you up to that supernatural place called HEAVEN and as you read, the very presence of that Holy place begins to invade your being! The wonders and majesty along with the fullness of love that you will discover within these pages will change you FOREVER! Get ready to know what our Lord has prepared for those who go home to Him; and what He is about to do with those who are still living in this day and hour! Heaven has begun to invade our lives on earth and will continue to do so at an accelerated rate!

When someone who has accepted Christ dies, their spirit leaves it's body, a transport to Heaven will be waiting with their guardian angel(s) and sometimes the Lord himself will be there. After an amazing journey beyond the planets, solar systems and places yet undiscovered by human eyes, you will approach Heaven. It will be the most brilliant, glorious place which causes all other beauty to fade from memory. When you first arrive, Angels will be everywhere and the splendor of it all will stun you to the point that you think you are walking in a dream. You pass by a flower bed (some of them possibly suspended in air) and they begin to sing to you as they change into colors that do not exist on earth. The atmosphere is so PURE and joy floods your being as you realize it is real. Jesus comes (you will gaze at him for some time) and after filling you with His love, will escort you to the Throne Room and up the steps until you stand before the Father. Engulfed in His arms, you will know that you are finally HOME and that you never want to be without Him again. Everywhere you go in Heaven you are accepted and loved; even if someone, while on earth, may have been your enemy at one time.

Your mansion has been wonderfully and perfectly made to your exact desire; even the décor inside has been considered. This will include supernatural things as a part of your home, such as a waterfall cascading inside or flowers growing right out of the walls. They will also prepare the property your mansion sits upon and if there is something you always desired to do on earth but were never able to, I am certain it has been incorporated into your dwelling.

For example, if you always wanted a horse, you would not just have one, but a huge stable of them. However, they will never be a burden to care for, they will cost nothing to feed, never get dirty, never be ill tempered nor sick; just a pleasure to own. It will be their greatest desire to please you and all your friends who will come to ride with you! There is a strong possibility you may have some that fly too.

One of the most significant differences is that everyone living in Heaven shares their gifts and talents with one another, without cost to anyone! That means that if you were an artist on earth, your mansion would include a fully furnished studio (with unlimited supplies) to produce the art and a gallery to show your work. People come to your gallery to view the masterpieces you create and you 'give' them away. You paid nothing to produce them, so charge nothing in return. You will never have to pay for anything you receive in Heaven and actually, they do not even use money! Everything is FREE!

When you go to Heaven, one of the most enjoyable things you do is go 'shopping' for gifts and then put them in the mansions of those who are yet to depart from earth. Upon the arrival of friends and family from earth, and after their greeting in the Throne Room by the Father, you will have an amazing 'welcome home' celebration for them in their mansion.

One thing everyone is interested in is if you eat in Heaven and the answer is YES. Not because you have to, but we love to eat. The good news is that there will be NO weight gain or food allergies so everyone will enjoy eating in Heaven! The food does not come from animals that must be killed, but it is made from light (like many things in Heaven), however, food tastes and smells so much better up there; steak, pizza, chicken, fruits, vegetable dishes and of course the DESSERTS! Whatever it is that you like to eat is so good, it almost 'calls' to you! The cinnamon rolls are the size of dinner plates and the pizzas are the size of the tables they are served on! People have gifts as chefs, so there are many restaurants to visit and enjoy with family and friends.

God has caught me up hundreds of times to Heaven and I am always awestruck by the beauty and life that exists there. There are many wonderful things apparent to your eyes, but there is still an unseen realm within that realm. It has to do with the fact that in Heaven there is not only no 'time' as we know it, but there is also no 'space' either. What I mean is, that on earth (a physical realm) it is only possible to have one thing taking up a fixed amount of space, however, in Heaven (which is a spirit realm) it is possible for more than one thing to exist in the same space. It is very hard to explain if you have not experienced being there. For example you could be walking through Heaven and come upon a family enjoying a picnic in a beautiful setting and right next to them is a door that is suspended with no apparent building attached to it and yet, if you enter through the door, you will be in a totally different area or place in Heaven. How amazing is that!

God has so many fantastic things to see and do in Heaven, but something everyone enjoys is the Portal. This was created so everyone living in Heaven could go there and see and hear their family members on earth. It states in Hebrews 12:1 that there is a great cloud of witnesses that have passed on before us, that would be those who have departed this earth upon dying and now live in Heaven. They can go to the Portal whenever they wish and will usually lean over the balcony and begin declaring God's will over our life.There is an amazing city area in Heaven and I have included an illustration of a street scene there. I was taken to this particular street to see a movie production studio, a gemologist who was a jeweler in Heaven and to view people using the Transport Kiosk to 'instantly' travel to another part of Heaven. The movie studio was built at the end of someone's beautiful mansion and the name suspended on top of that building was LPP (Little Papa Productions). The other business I passed by was a jeweler from Israel and his building was in the shape of a huge gemstone. As you approached, a facet would lower its self down and allow people to enter into the showroom. In this shop, you can select from the jewelry already created or you may custom order some for friends or family. Further down that street are places to get perfumes and oils or fabrics so dazzling they could only be created in Heaven. This beautiful street in Heaven was bordered by the Crystal Sea, where I watched brilliant light rays shoot forth from it. I have told many people about the Crystal Sea and that it looks like a million diamonds were dropped into it.

It is an honor to share this revelation of Heaven and even though I did not die to go there, I must 'die to myself' every day to reveal His mysteries! God will entrust His secrets to His friends, those who have surrendered everything and those who are willing to live a holy life. You cannot be afraid of the face of man if you are to boldly proclaim what God has said or what He has shown you! In these last days, God will be catching more people up so they can testify about the divine place called Heaven. Just be certain you belong to Christ because when you die; whomever owns you, comes for you!

Street Scene in Heaven

CHAPTER TWO

The Streets of Gold and where they take you

⪫⭤•⊙•⭤⪪

Yes, they really are made of gold and God used it so we would have the best just to walk on! Perhaps one of the most asked questions I get, besides the mansions, is about the streets of gold; they want to know what they look like. They have a transparent quality about them because they were created to reflect the glory of God; which causes them to have a beautiful golden glow. Yes, you can actually see yourself (even though it is your spirit being) when you look down at them. The streets go all over Heaven and besides leading you to mansions; they take you to many wonderful places God created for you to enjoy.

I have walked upon the streets of gold many times and I promise you, our Father in Heaven truly gives us the desire of our hearts. Sometimes, they will begin to 'move' you along to your destination while you are walking on them. They can take you to the mansions but can also go to the Hall of Wisdom, Word University, or the Body Parts Warehouse. Some of the fun places they carry you, are the Amusement Park or Surf Park the Lord and His Father created for your pleasure. You must keep reminding yourself that Heaven is a supernatural place and therefore, things that would be impossible on earth, are possible in Heaven. Like the 'roads of pure light' which come, pick you up and 'express' you above the ground to many places.

Many forms of transportation travel upon the streets; such as chariots, motorcycles with hyperdrive, carriages of all types and even antique cars or trolleys. There are also the 'high tech' modes of travel such as star cruisers or the 'Transport Kiosks' that are located on the streets of God. You step into one and are instantly taken on rays of light to some other part of Heaven. The children ride on hover boards without any concern of falling off or getting lost. The only fuel used in Heaven besides the wind, is light. Light in Heaven, is a 'substance' things are made out of, such as food, clothing and even fuel.

On earth, we have only just begun to understand the value of light and its uses.

Some of the places you are taken by the streets in Heaven would be the many mansions God has prepared for His people. They are made in many different styles, because we are all different. I have seen mansions built along the Crystal Sea and in the middle of it on a beautiful island. There are also those that look like gemstones with many facets in them and they are located along the cliffs of the Valley of the Falls. This place is located beyond the Mountains of Spices mentioned in Song of Solomon and there are 50 waterfalls cascading into this gorgeous valley. Your mansion is created to turn slowly so that you always have a view of the valley.

However, some of the most fascinating mansions are the Sky Mansions, which tower above the others. These mansions are very modern or futuristic in design and are supported by a huge see-thru column which is the entrance that you step into and just 'say' what floor you wish to go to. You are then propelled upward through the tube-like column and arrive at the floor of your choice! Most of these mansions are are about 80 feet up into the sky of Heaven and when you step out on the third story deck, WOW, you can see everything. Most of the walls are see-through so that you miss nothing and you have easy access to the star cruiser parked outside on your personal landing pad! I was so captivated by them that I chose to include them as one of the illustrations in the book. I tell people if you really want to see what one is like; watch an old JETSONS cartoon and they will give you an idea of what I was shown in Heaven!

Of course, there are also many fun places that the streets of Gold take you to, and some are discussed in other chapters of this book.

The Sky Mansion

CHAPTER THREE

Higher Education

><-<>-O-<>-<

WORD UNIVERSITY

Most people will be surprised to know that you will be educated in Heaven. There are several reasons for this, one being the fact that all must know the scriptures.

If you do not learn the Word of God on earth, you will learn it in Heaven! That is why they created 'WORD UNIVERSITY'! You will go there and be taught the 'revealed' word of God, not just a head knowledge which brings no life. Many of the people I saw teaching the revealed word, were young people whose students were many of the professors of earth's universities. God qualifies according to the 'heart' of man, not by the world's standards.

I remember it well when I was taken several years ago. So much excitement in the air around that place, as many of the redeemed were going in and out of the building. The architecture reminded me of some of the great universities in Europe. Everyone could hardly wait to receive the revealed word of God.

Some of the classes were held outside under the trees and some inside, but the structure of the classrooms was very different than our universities. All of the seating was very relaxed, not rigid and uncomfortable. One of the rooms I was shown had seating that resembled large bean bag chairs but it appeared that they were filled with some type of liquid. The professor, who was a youth, was instructing them in the book of Isaiah. They were sitting in a circle, captivated by the words he spoke about the prophet's writings. At some point during your instruction of the various books in the Bible, the author of that particular book would also instruct the class. How would you like to be taught by Isaiah or David or even Paul? Pretty fantastic isn't it, but that is what Heaven is! Some of the rooms had no ceiling and open to the outside. All of the walls in the rooms were embellished with scenes from the Bible and when you stood in front of them, the scenes came to life! I would not be surprised if people took the course several times at Word University!

How wonderful if we as Believers could feel the same way. We must all be aware that we will never live a victorious life on earth unless we are grounded in the Holy Bible. Even though it is pleasurable to soak in the presence of God, worship together with other Believers, have divine encounters, it cannot replace the necessity of studying His Word! When you do not have a solid foundation in the Word, you can be deceived by the enemy (Satan) and your prayers will have no real power in them (they will be spoken from an un-renewed mind). If you are continually under attack and nothing ever goes right in your life, get into the Word and find out what Christ said to do. It would also help to read and meditate on the book of James, which teaches you how important the words are that come out of your mouth. Words create, so what are you creating with yours?

God's Word is precious to those that love Him, it is the story of His creation, His people, His love for us and eternity! Please make time for it in your life!

ROYAL UNIVERSITY

Another reason for education and training is because as the Word declares, we will rule and reign with Christ! God is not going to put you over a territory and stick a scepter in your hand and say, "Go for it"! You actually receive training to lead using the Love, knowledge and understanding of Heaven!

Part of this training is given by Michael, the Archangel who commands the armies of Heaven. God's leaders in eternity will be filled with His Glory and operate in absolute love, freedom and grace. What a relief that we will be fully supplied and equipped for our eternal existence.

The architecture of this university was similar to that of a castle. I was intrigued by the beautifully woven tapestries that filled the hallways and the stream of water which was running right down the middle of it. As you passed by the murals decorating some of the walls, they 'came to life'; it was captivating! I am continually made aware of the fact that Heaven is a 'supernatural' place. No one could possibly be bored living there.

There are many levels to progress through until you successfully complete their Leadership course.

The ultimate goal is to be like Christ, becoming a servant leader. You will portray the Father's heart at all times and learn many new ways to express His love to others. One thing you will never have to be concerned with or receive training in is how to defend your land! There will be no evil in eternity and Jesus will be the sole ruler sitting on the throne in the new earth (Revelation 22)!

At the end of this course, they have a huge celebration with much pageantry. It is a wonderful experience to be trained in Heaven as they have no failures! You will be filled with wisdom, knowledge and love; ready to rule and reign with our King, Jesus!

CREATION LAB

Then there is Creation Lab, one of my favorite places to visit! So many amazing things take place there, one being the ability to stand on a platform and (in hologram form) watch as God creates the original earth. He has recorded the history of the earth so that we may see 'significant events' as they took place; like the time the dinosaurs roamed and how the Ice Age came to be.

I will never forget the day I was caught up and allowed to experience this amazing place. The domed building had many facets in its architecture that gave it a reflective quality. It was emerald in color, with copper highlights. It is a place where you can go and view creation as God unveiled it from the beginning and a place you practice creating with the creator.

There is no visible entrance, but you must use your faith and words to create it. It is very difficult to explain exactly how you do it, but when you get there yourself, you will understand. I would rather take the space here to tell you what I saw when I stepped into the main room and the world we call Earth was born!

First you have to create an entrance to the building by using your faith. This took me a while, but I finally got inside. As I stood in the middle of the room, a platform began to rise up under my feet as excitement rose up in me. A beautiful light came from up above and showered the room in a brilliant hologram. The scene was so real, that I thought if I reached out, I could touch it. God appeared, and the Glory was so great, at first I had to close my eyes and then He began to speak to the void of space and suddenly things began to form and spin in the space (Genesis 1:1). Eventually, the earth appeared and God poured water out of His hand to measure out the ocean. I say 'ocean' because there was only one land mass on the original earth and water surrounded it on all sides. Then He spoke and amazing, strange plants were formed and put into place. The trees were huge, as were the flowers on this new earth. Some blooms were the size of a three story house and the aroma was intoxicating. How fun it was to see God create the different creatures and put them in the sea.

He was about to create more animals, but did something else first, He created an atmosphere in which they could live. He spoke and a transparent shield appeared far above in the sky. This shield went completely around the world and covered the whole earth, like a huge bubble. Next, He did an unexpected thing and called forth billions of gallons of water to cover the entire area of the shield. What power that took to put it in place and yet, not one drop goes spinning off into space. Then He called forth a second layer to the shield and placed it over the water to seal it in place. They called it a Water

Vapor Shield; which caused a continual heavy mist to come from the shield down onto the earth.

Then the Father began to create some of the strangest creatures that ever walked this planet – the dinosaurs! Some were skinny and small, about six feet high and then there were those that towered 90 feet high. The continuous mist was necessary to keep the skin of the dinosaurs from cracking and falling off. God continued to create many other creatures like birds that made beautiful sounds and many kinds of fish for the sea. The wonderful thing was that they all lived in harmony with each other, because as in the Garden of Eden, evil had not entered in. How perfect everything was and the sky was a peachy, rosy color; not blue. This effect was created from the water vapor shield and the light above it, filtering through.

Planet Earth looked like a beautiful, multi-colored marble out in space and peace remained (millions of years) until the day everything changed! There was war in Heaven and for the first time, lightening struck the earth with a loud clap! Michael had just kicked Lucifer out of Heaven and he came streaking down to earth. This continued to happen for some time as one third of the angels (whom Lucifer had deceived) were also kicked out of the celestial realm, never to return. Although they were condemned to Hell (in the center of the earth) they eventually began to come to the surface of earth and defile it. This caused an upheaval on the planet and life was never the same again. Satan (formerly Lucifer) was furious about his failed plan to exalt himself over God's throne and so decided to take over this new earth! It says in Jeremiah 4, that he began to make the earth a wilderness. Evil then entered into the creatures God had made; they became vicious and began to turn from their original state and instead of eating the grasses and fruit, they ate each other! The beautiful earth, now being controlled by Lucifer became defiled.

Time passed and when God had enough of the destruction, He did something to stop Lucifer; He caused the Ice Age! I was truly captivated, standing and watching as the mysteries of the ages unfolded before me. At the same time, a little overwhelmed because of the level of revelation being given to me. All of a sudden, I saw the Father reach across space and break the water vapor shield and billions of gallons of water hit the earth. Wham! There went the one land mass, into many pieces, floating across the sea. Some of them overlapping upon each other and burying many of the dinosaurs between layers of earth. Some of the now new continents formed massive mountains, which at the same time caused deep valleys to form. The water kept coming, until all the earth was completely covered. Then God leaned forward again and blew onto the earth; immediately ice began to form over the surface of the waters and life stopped as the earth, covered in darkness, entered into the Ice Age!

The scene changed (millions of years later as the earth lie dormant under the ice) and I saw streaks of light come from Heaven and the Spirit of God was hovering over the frozen planet, waiting. Then I saw God lean forward and He blew upon the ice and instantly the earth was defrosted. Once again, water covered the whole earth (Gen. 1:2) and there was no land mass visible to the eye. God spoke again and light was! It was so fantastic, as I watched God re-create the earth, different atmosphere, animals and even man, but eventually they sent me back down to earth. If you accept Christ and make it to Heaven; you can go to Creation Lab and see this too.

Pursuing Knowledge

There are other places in Heaven where you can pursue knowledge or wisdom. I was recently taken to one of those places; they called it the Hall of Knowledge. It was thrilling as you traveled across Heaven on a road of light to get there. I could see this structure from some distance, both because of the tremendous size and the glow from the Glory of God that emanated from it. As I entered I could see staggered rows of tall diamond-like towers containing innumerable volumes. The road continued to travel up and down these towers until I located the volume I desired. As soon as I removed it from the niche, a pedestal table 'appeared' in front of me and as I opened the faceted case of the book, a hologram appeared and I 'watched' the book instead of reading it! The Father has allowed me to include an illustration of this amazing place, where information is kept on almost any subject (nothing evil or unclean) you could desire to know more about!

How wonderful of the Father to allow us to have access to more knowledge, wisdom and understanding when we get to Heaven. My favorite, was 'understanding' because that is knowledge of the

Holy One! Although everyone in Heaven enjoys the corporate time spent together in the Throne Room with the Father and Jesus; there will still be those that have an intense desire to have some 'alone' time with them too. Those who pursued a deeper relationship like this on earth will not be disappointed when they get to Heaven! There are special gardens created where you can meet with the Lord and only you and He have a key; so you can visit with Him whenever you desire. He wants to spend time with you too so you may know the love that was in His heart when He died for you!

Every Believer should desire to know Him and as you pursue that, you will begin to hear and know Him! If you want this desire, but do not feel it is possible; ask Him to give it to you and He will! The Father calls us His 'offspring' and Christ gave His life for us; they DO want you to know them!

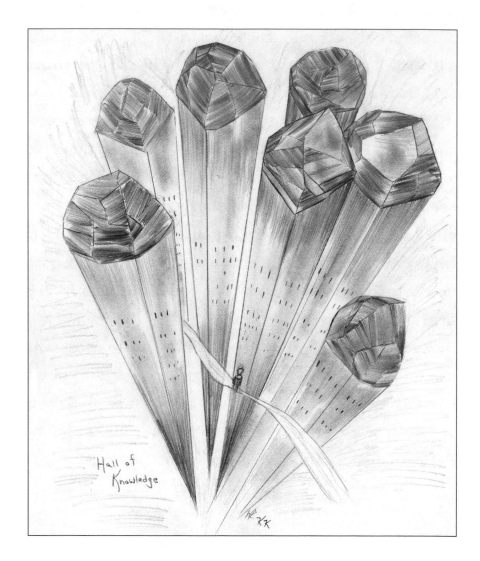

The Hall of Knowledge

CHAPTER FOUR

Dearly Departed – Living in the Celestial City

>━┼━◆━━◯━━◆━┼━◄

As in Volume I, you will learn about actual people who have departed and are now living in Heaven. At the end of each story, you will find a written statement by a family member(s) or friends whose lives were dramatically changed when this information was shared with them. Never, at any time have I spoken with any of the people living in Heaven; I was taken only to observe. None of them were aware of my presence nor did they attempt to converse with me. The Holy Spirit catches me up by my spirit at the will of the Father and when they are ready for me to return, they simply send me back. I am continually overwhelmed that they trust me to share about that holy, amazing place! The following two stories will inspire and bless you as you get a glimpse of life in Heaven.

SURVILLA'S HOMECOMING

This event takes place in 2000 when the Lord showed me the future mansion of Survilla, Patricia Aldridge's mother. Although I knew Patricia, and her daughter, Cheryl; I did not know her mother, who lived in Tennessee. The Holy Spirit caught me up and showed me this beautiful Victorian home that was three stories high and had a huge wrap-around porch just made for entertaining. The grounds were breathtaking and included meadows filled with flowers, a stream that ran through her property with a waterfall and a footbridge at the back of her home where birds were singing everywhere. The flowers had amazing aromas and the trees bore many types of fruit. She had a long circular drive, also with many types of flowering bushes on either side.

The beautiful mansion was white with a blue roof and had intricate detailing on the gingerbread crown molding. There were many floor-to-ceiling windows in this mansion, each floor being about 30 feet high. On the top floor I was shown her dining room which would seat approximately 60 people. Even the design in the wood of her table was wonderful to look at and the gloss of the wood reflected the beauty of the huge chandelier suspended above it. The table was set with gold and white china made by a fine craftsman. The entire third floor was surrounded with windows so that her guests could enjoy the view of her property which had been so lovingly created. The open windows allowed a light breeze to billow the fine fabric of the draperies, which had a border of pearls on them. Live flowers were growing right out of the walls, which emitted intoxicating aromas. What a divine atmosphere to enjoy the pleasure of fellowship in!

Entering onto the ground floor, with its grand staircase, were many rooms filled with beautiful furnishings. Then I saw something that really surprised me; it was a big kitchen with many gadgets and equipment I could not identify. There were also many marble counters to prepare meals on. I did notice that the appliances had no visible means of energy with which to operate them. In other words, all equipment and/or appliances work and run because they exist within the realm of Heaven. Wow, they will never break down, need repairing or have to be replaced! I was told that one of Survilla's favorite things was to cook and entertain family and friends. Well, I am positive she will enjoy creating many meals in this kitchen.

Usually, in Heaven, you merely sit down and order what you want and it appears on your table in front of you. Once finished with your meal, it all disappears; there is NOTHING to clean up – PRAISE GOD!!!

Her home was almost complete and I was told it was only a short while before she was to come home to Heaven. They brought me back outside and showed me a large piece of her land being tilled. I asked what it was for and I was told. "It is for her vegetable garden, she loves to grow them. Everyone will want her vegetables as she will grow the best in Heaven"! The best part about growing anything in Heaven is that after you pull your hands from the dirt, they are instantly clean. Why do you think they call it 'Heaven'?

The last thing I was shown was the two children waiting on the steps of the mansion. It was a boy and a girl and I was even told their names, Cynthia and Edward. Their faces were filled with joy and anticipation of Survilla's homecoming and although

I was not told who they were, I was certain they were her children! How wonderful of the Father to reunite children to their parents; where they will grow very slowly and develop every gift God gave them. I could hardly wait to call my friend and tell her all I was shown.

<u>*Patricia Aldridge's Personal Statement, November 18, 2010*</u>

My home is in upstate New York, but early in December of 2000 my husband, Grant, and I were in Tennessee at my mother's house preparing to spend some time in Florida. Something came up and I was delayed leaving, so our daughter, Cheryl, offered to take my mom on home with her as all the family planned to go to her home for Christmas.

Before I arrived in Florida I received a phone call from Cheryl, telling me that Mother came to her one morning saying that someone came into her bedroom and told her she was going home soon. This concerned Cheryl and so she called her friend Kat and asked her to pray about it.

As she began to pray, God caught her up and showed her mother's home in Heaven. Kat wrote the account down for me. I was amazed as I read the description. Kat, who did not know my mom, had described exactly what Mother would like! The house was big with a large dining room (Kat later told me it would seat 60 people)!

There were many people waiting to greet her and were going to have a celebration when she arrived, but they were "waiting for her to cook part of the meal because she loved to cook!" I knew that mother loved to cook, but to cook in Heaven?... So one day I casually said to her, "Mother, do you want to cook when you get to Heaven?" With no hesitation, she briskly replied, "Well, it wouldn't be Heaven if I couldn't cook!" I recalled that as I was growing up, it was not unusual to have 20 – 30 people at our house for Sunday dinner.

Besides loving to cook, mother also loved to garden. She definitely had a 'green thumb'. Not only did she enjoy growing the vegetables, she enjoyed looking at gardening catalogs and reading the gardening magazines during the winter months. So it was no surprise that Kat saw some ground being tilled on my Mother's property in Heaven so she could grow vegetables.

One thing that did puzzle me a bit was when Kat said the house was blue & white because all the colors Mom decorated with were greens, yellows, beiges with accents of orange. So one day I said to her, "Mother, what is your favorite color?" She hesitated and replied, "Well, I guess it's blue". So much for my observation! She now has a beautiful mansion with a blue roof, her favorite color!

The description of the grounds around her mansion is certainly something my mom would like. The meadow like landscape, with flowers, a flowing stream and the birds that would not eat her vegetables, just sing to her.

When Kat first mentioned the two children I was a little confused as I was not raised with other siblings. Then the Holy Spirit reminded me that my mother had experienced a still birth and a miscarriage. One was before my birth and the other after my birth. I knew these were the two children Kat had seen waiting on the mansion steps. It was overwhelming when I realized she had just described my brother and sister who are living in Heaven.

The message given to me by Kat has been such a comfort and joy since my Mother departed this past January. We shared the story about her mansion in Heaven at the service and have shared it many times since then. People are always captivated by the story of Survilla's home going! I will always be grateful to God for blessing Kat with Heaven's revelation and for allowing her to share it with me!

Mrs. Mac's Studio

Several years ago, there was a 93 year old woman affectionately known as "Mrs. Mac". She was Scottish and had outlived several husbands but now was unable to care for herself. It was said that she was quite opinionated but extremely interesting to talk to.

Problems developed when she became ill and had to go to the emergency room several times. Each time, her care-giver, Patricia, would call and ask me if Mrs. Mac was going to recover. Some people are well aware of my experiences in Heaven and felt I had a 'hot line' to get such information passed on to me. The funny thing is, each time the Lord did tell me she would recover.

A few months passed and one day the Lord told me, "Mrs. Mac will be coming home soon, her home is completely ready but we are finishing the studio for her students." I asked him, "What studio?" He then showed me a beautiful place filled with pianos and one great 'grand' piano. I could not wait to call Patricia and tell her what I had seen. I asked her, "Did Mrs. Mac play or teach piano?" She replied, "Her mother actually wanted her to learn the violin, but her greatest desire was to play the piano. Her father owned a grand piano and decided one day she would learn to play by herself. She did teach herself and became so good, that she was asked to play at weddings, for her church and even offered free lessons. Her favorite students were children, because she had none of her own; although she always wanted some". When I shared my experience with her, she was blessed at what was being prepared in Heaven for Mrs. Mac.

Another time I was shown a little girl (about age 4) waiting on the steps of Mrs. Mac's mansion. She had long red hair, pulled up to a pony tail and had a beautiful smile! I wondered who she was, as I had been told Mrs. Mac had no children even though she had been married several times. As soon as I got a chance, I called Patricia and had her ask Mrs. Mac if she ever lost a baby through miscarriage. Her reply gave me hope as Mrs. Mac told her, although there was never any proof she had ever been pregnant, the desire to have a child never left her. What a surprise she would have, when I told Patricia about the little girl I had seen in Heaven.

It was a short time after this that Mrs. Mac had taken a turn for the worse and they were calling in 'hospice'. The Lord did permit time for Patricia to tell her good-bye (she had grown very fond of her). She called to tell me when she departed, but I already knew; I was allowed to see her leave on the transport when it came to pick her up. It was wonderful to not only see the ship, but the two angels who were escorting her. Mrs. Mac looked amazingly beautiful although minutes before she had been very old. Her spirit is eternally young and now she is living an awesome life in Heaven with her little girl, whom I was told she named, Alicia May!

Statement from Mrs.Mac's caregiver, Patricia, 11-28-10

I am so grateful that God allowed me to care for Mrs. Mac, who I grew very fond of in the months prior to her death. The revelations about her mansion in Heaven that Kat shared with me have given me such comfort and peace. I was amazed at the detail God gave her and the fact that Kat had no idea Mrs. Mac could even play the piano and yet saw a 'studio' filled with pianos in her mansion. Even though I miss her, I know that Mrs. Mac is enjoying her life teaching children to play the piano. How wonderful that the Father allows us to use our gifts and even fulfills our desires when we get to Heaven.

Mrs. Mac always wanted a child and now she has her own little girl; it thrills me to think of them spending the rest of their lives together. I look forward to the day that I too will live in Heaven and can go and visit Mrs. Mac and meet her little girl. I pray everyone who reads this, will have a desire to know and allow Jesus to become the Lord of their life! I thank God for allowing Kat to share all that she was told and shown regarding Mrs. Mac's heavenly home; I will never forget it!

CHAPTER FIVE

Living Worship – In Heaven, In Earth

＞—＋＜＞—◯—＜＞＋—＜

It is one of the most exciting places to be in Heaven, the Throne Room of God with all the Redeemed (those Believers who died and are living in Heaven) worshipping and dancing. I am going to try and describe some of the things I witnessed during several of my visits to the Throne Room. The throne is high and lifted up as it says in the Word and it is in the center of the room, not at the back wall. This made it possible for all the people to be near the Father and Jesus (he sits at the right hand of God). There are four sets of steps that go up to the throne so that at any time they wish, the redeemed can run right up and visit.

One of the most beautiful things I remember is the rainbow around the throne which goes in a huge circle from the floor up to the ceiling and back around; totally engulfing the throne in radiant, amazing colors. The outermost band of color in this rainbow is purple and then next is a brilliant sapphire blue and after that a gorgeous teal (the widest band) and then sometimes the colors change after that. At times when I was there, the other bands of color are just like a normal rainbow as seen on earth. But sometimes, it will be a thin band of emerald green, then topaz gold and finally the glorious white that emanates from the face of God! Standing in that Glory, which is the love He has for all of His children will cause you to be permanently undone.

There are other thrones encircling God's throne (the twenty-four elders), but the most noticeable thing are the Living Creatures! Amazing beings, who are not animals that walk on all fours, but are intelligent beings that walk upright like us. They have gossamer garments and, through them, you see hundreds of eyes looking back at you. They also have six wings, which have eyes in all the feathers (every eye moves independently of each other). One has the head of a lion, another head of an ox, one the head of an eagle and one the head of a man; all are extremely intelligent and will be used during the end time outpouring. When they declare, "HOLY, HOLY, HOLY" the room shakes with the power in their words. Smoke (which is the glory cloud) and fire with lightening pour out from the throne of God.

Worship in the throne room is not easy to describe as it involves music and beings that do not exist on this earth. The Seraphim, have blue fire coming from the top of their heads, fly back and forth over top of the Father as He sits on his throne; these are powerful beings involved with the worship and are in close proximity to the one who sits upon the throne. On earth, they hover over those who minister to the Lord during worship and release Glory upon them. Many people there create and use banners and flags to demonstrate their passion for the Father and Jesus. As they run with the banners across the floor, the image on the banner comes to life! If it is a lion, it begins to roar loudly from the fabric or if it is a trumpet or shofars, they begin to sound out, worshipping along with the redeemed! The Glory becomes so rich and heavy that everyone ends up on their faces, soaking in the love that comes in waves from the Father's heart.

Our worship on earth is collected and presented in the Throne Room as incense. The sweet aromas continually fill that place as we love God with our song, instruments and dance. If you could see into the spirit realm around you as you worship, it would amaze you. Some people have been given a 'seer' anointing by the Holy Spirit which enables them to do that and since God chose me to be one of them, I can tell you what happens. When you dance before the Lord in worship, the angels come from Heaven and place a 'spiritual' canvas under your feet. As you worship, your feet begin to paint a masterpiece with your love and when completed, that masterpiece is presented before the throne of God and then placed in your Praise Gallery. This is a place with your name on it; it was made just to hold all the things you create as worship for your God. When you get to Heaven you will enjoy going there to see the many precious things God collected from your life as worship to Him.

When you sing, in the spirit realm, ribbons of beautiful color stream from your mouth and these begin to 'weave' a tapestry which also becomes a masterpiece of your love. The same thing happens when you play an instrument; it creates a tapestry of worship. These tapestries will also be placed in your praise gallery. Many prophetic psalmists are now being 'caught' up as God is opening their eyes to see what is being created through worship. When you get to Heaven and begin to worship (from any place around Heaven) you are literally caught up and ride on your worship across the sky which takes you directly to the Throne Room. What an amazing thing to experience while living there.

If you are an artist and paint a masterpiece, in the spirit realm, every time you move the paintbrush, you release music notes from it. By the time you are finished with your artwork; you have created a 'symphony' that is captured, played in the throne room and placed in your praise gallery. When you get there one day and stand before the masterpiece you painted, you will actually hear the music your love created at the same time.

Our worship becomes a weapon as it passes right through satan's realm (the second heaven) on the way to the Throne Room. It sends spiritual missiles which do great damage to his property. They have to patch and repair a lot when we passionately worship our Lord! Read Psalms 149, which says when dance, song & instruments are done as worship, it binds the enemy in fetters of iron!

Yes, you can actually do damage to the devil's domain by worshipping God and especially when you are going through a trial. When you choose to worship instead of crying and complaining, you release GREAT love and power through your praise. Even King David, knew praise released power and that was why he always sent the dancers and singers out ahead of His armies. The battle was already won through the worship of the people. God loves it when we choose to praise; and, He will begin to move Heaven and Earth to intervene on your behalf. When we do a 'clap' offering for the Lord; it sends earthquakes through the second Heaven and demons scream in terror. Praise releases love for our God, but it also releases power!!

NEVER worship the same way again, do it with passion to Love Him and do it with Power to become a weapon in your God's hand!!

CHAPTER SIX

Kids in the Kingdom – the Babies Play Pond

>─┤◆>─◦──<◆├─<

When I was taken to this delightful place, I could not resist drawing it. There were all these adorable little babies playing together with the bunnies, turtles and butterflies. The babies were having so much fun and never had a care about getting hurt or lost. They never had to have an adult or what we would call a 'responsible' person with them because in Heaven you are always safe. The Father created this place so even the 'little' babies could enjoy themselves. He even has special miniature daises grown so they can pick them with their tiny hands.

This little pond filled with the light of God provides many fun things for these babies; they even slide down real rainbows! The deer come and give them rides as do the kangaroos; they also ride on the turtles in the pond or swim with the goldfish under water. When it is time to return to the nurseries, dragonflies are sent to deliver the message. The ones I saw were black and had red wings with jewel tone colors that reflected God's glory everywhere they went. They would land on the little baby's hands and announce that it was time to return to the nurseries because Jesus was coming. What a scene to see all the little animals carrying these precious little (miscarried or aborted) babies back to have a party with Jesus. I wanted you to see the joy they get to experience while living in Heaven.

There are many other places where children get to play and do amazing things with their friends; some look like places on earth and some are extraordinary. No child is ever left alone and many of them are living with other family members while waiting for their parents to arrive. Although no one is married in Heaven, you will live right next door to each other and have the pleasure of sharing the raising of your children. I explained in Revealing Heaven Volume I, how God allows families to stay connected in Heaven so you do things and go places together. Although we are all one big family in Heaven, you never forget those who were your family members on Earth. You will be known as you were known on earth, so people will recognize you; only you will be perfect in every way!

There are testimonies of people being taken to Heaven and allowed to see their children. Most of the time, they looked exactly the same age as when they passed on to Heaven. If you lost a baby, that baby will be exactly the age you want it to be when you arrive yourself. The best news is, NO diaper changes or all night feedings; even the little babies talk, walk, play and need no continual care – just hugs, love and lots of fun! They all know who their parents are, so if you aborted (repent for it) or miscarried a baby; please name it. If you do not know if it was a boy or girl; just pick a name for either one and they will have a ceremony where they will be presented with the name you chose for them!

Our loving God does not let any child miss their destiny or miss using their gifts. They will be raised in the most holy, loving atmosphere; waiting for the day when they can be with you and be with you through eternity. We are all eternal beings and can never 'cease' to exist; so be sure you know where you will be spending eternity! It will be Heaven where everyone will love you; or Hell & death, where no one will love you! Choose LIFE!

BABIES PLAY POND

CHAPTER SEVEN

Stones of Fire – the Ancient Paths

➤⦿➤◆➤⦿➤◆➤⦿➤◆⦿

This chapter will truly unveil one of the greatest mysteries man has enquired about. Where did we come from? It will also reveal what the 'Stones of Fire' were that you can read about in Ezekiel 28, and why Lucifer said he was 'like' the Most High! Also, it will be revealed what the Father showed me when He caught me up to his throne on February 17, 2010. It changes forever what you think about your past and especially, your future! So come, and walk upon the Ancient Paths, where every person who ever existed played, before being sent to earth!

The ancient paths are not some place in past history, or even some pretty place in Heaven. They are inside the Father, where all life, love, creation, revelation and eternity come from. If you could step inside the Father, you would see a beautiful place, not organs like in a man. He is the eternal God and inside of Him is eternity. It is in that beautiful place inside God that we all came from before being sent to earth. Psalms 139 states: He knew us before we began to breathe and He wrote every day of our life before we were born. Also in Jeremiah 1:5 it says, He knew us before He formed us in our mother's womb. The Word also says He is our Father and we are His offspring, in other words, 'we came from Him'. In Acts 17:28, it states: .. in Him we move, we lived, we had our 'being' or existence and that prophets of old spoke of this, we are His offspring. God is also called 'the Father of <u>spirits</u>' (Hebrews 12:9, KJV); those spirits would be you and me before we were born into this earth.

Sometimes when I am caught up to the throne and standing before the Father, I can see little spirits flowing in and out of the Glory that comes from His being. They are all saying the same thing, "Send me, please send me". They do not yet have a real body so cannot exist outside the Father.

Once He sends them to earth and they are placed in a womb at the time of conception; they become a living human being! God did not create the earth and then decide to have a family; he created the earth so He could send us there to be born and become a family that could live with him and not just in Him. Then when man fell through sin in the Garden of Eden, He sent His son to pay a price through death so that He could bring us back to Him. In the beginning, we lived inside God; then He sent us to earth so He could live in us (through Christ) and then in eternity, we would all live together.

Now that I have established the fact that inside the Father is a beautiful place, I can reveal about the stones of fire. I have known for some time that they were inside God, not some place in Heaven. The Father had told me they were at the very heart of His being, where all life, creation, love, revelation, wealth and even eternity came from. He had also told me that was where Lucifer had walked, inside him. He had revealed to me several years ago that besides Jesus and the Holy Spirit, only the archangels had access to step inside God. This created a very intimate relationship with their creator and revealed a level of trust beyond the norm.

In Ezekiel 28 it talks about the creation and fall of Lucifer and I will expound on those scriptures. This chapter was a Word from God to Lucifer spoken through God's prophet, Ezekiel. The Father is reminding Lucifer how he had created him to be the most beautiful cherub that 'covers' and how perfect he was in the day he made him. It mentions in verse 13 (KJV), "Thou hast been in Eden the garden of God; every precious stone was thy covering; the sardius, topaz and the diamond, the beryl, the onyx and the jasper, the sapphire, the emerald, and the carbuncle, and gold: the workmanship of thy tabrets and of thy pipes was prepared in thee the day that thou wast created. Lucifer was the only cherub that was decorated with gemstones, which made him the most beautiful in all of Heaven. He also was the only angelic being that could create something; music, from the pipes and tabrets God put in him. He was made this way so he could make music while the other angels worshipped God.

Then in verse 14 (KJV) it states, "Thou art the anointed cherub that covereth; and I have set thee so; thou wast upon the holy mount of God; thou hast walked up and down in the midst of the stones of fire. This shows that Lucifer was specially made for a specific purpose, to cover worship! He had the ability to step inside God, where the holy mount was and cover over the stones of fire (God's heart) and make music while the other angels worshipped. He stood there and felt all the worship as it entered into the heart (stones of fire) of God. After a while, He began to desire that worship for himself. After all, he was like God because he could create worship and he had unlimited access to the heart of God. He began to become puffed up and in verse 15 (KJV) it states, "Thou wast perfect in thy ways from the day that thou wast created, till iniquity was found in thee".

Lucifer began to go around Heaven and 'traffic' his wares (ability to create music and show off his beauty). Verse 16 says, "By the multitude of your merchandise they have filled the midst of thee with violence, and thou hast sinned; therefore I will cast thee as profane out of the mountain of God, and I will destroy (or keep) thee, O covering cherub, from the midst of the stones of fire". This meant when he was found with sin in his being, God kicked him out from himself and never gave him entrance again to His heart.

Another thing I want to mention is what Lucifer thought about himself after pride and sin entered him. In Isaiah 14: 13 (KJV), "I will exalt my throne above the stars of God, I will sit also upon the mount of the people, in the sides of the north; verse 14, ".....I will be like the Most High". This is Lucifer stating that He was more important than God himself and that he would be the one that would not just rule over Heaven, but even the 'people' or the spirits that lived inside God. There were no people living anywhere in Heaven at this point in time and it is not talking about 'created beings' like the angels. The 'people' are the spirits (us before coming to earth) who had not been born into the earth. Lucifer continually said he was 'like the Most High' and I know people think it was because he could create like God, but it was for another reason.

In January of this year, 2010, the Father told me He would show me how the rainbow (mentioned in Revelation 4) was generated from His being. I was very excited, but knew He would reveal this in His timing. Well, about a month later, on February 17th I was talking to the Father as soon as I woke up and was telling Him I wanted to know and see His heart. Although I was speaking symbolically, He took it literally and the next thing I heard was, "I will show you the stones of fire" (His heart). Before I could respond, He caught me up and I was standing on the third step down from His throne.

That was the only time I could not tell you what was going on in the throne room because I was so captivated by being that close to the Father. The waves of Love begin to pour into your being even seeming to replace the very air you breathe. It is as if you are breathing in His presence and once again you are a part of Him! There really is no earthly way to make you understand this, it is a supernatural experience; being one with Him. As I stood there, feeling like a little girl, the Father reached inside Himself and pulled out the biggest diamond I had ever seen. My eyes were then drawn to a blue fire that burned up and around this magnificent gemstone. What I noticed next caused my heart to leap; all around the stone a rainbow began to form due to the fire burning under and over this multifaceted diamond. The colors matched exactly the rainbow that at that very moment was being generated from the Father's being! I knew instantly how the Father's rainbow was made, from the Stones of Fire that burned with passionate fire in the heart of His being! Actually, this revelation proves that the stones of fire are gemstones and that they are inside the Father. Ask yourself what happens if you hold a gemstone or faceted crystal up to a bright light or flame; it causes a rainbow!

As I continued to stand there, the Holy Spirit whispered to me, "Did not Lucifer say, "I am like the Most High?" Suddenly, I understood why Lucifer kept saying those words; he had gemstones on the outside and he knew God had them on the inside! Wow, I realized God had given me the answer to one of the mysteries of God; Lucifer did resemble the Father because of the gemstones! He fell because he had access to go in and out whenever it pleased him, he became puffed up because of his beauty and his ability to create like God. It destroyed his chance of living in eternity with the Father and since he was a 'created' being, he could never repent from that sin!

My attention was drawn back to the Father as He began to quote scripture, "On this rock, I will build my church" and then "You shall become precious, living stones" and He continued, "you will shine like the stars in the Heavens". He kept quoting scripture for some time and then began sharing about gemstones on earth and in Heaven. These are some of the things He mentioned: the gems in the vest of the high priest, the gemstones He is dropping into meetings all over the world (because they represent

His heart), the diamonds in the 'Crystal Sea', the foundation 'stones' of the New Jerusalem, the robes we will receive in Heaven are embellished with gems every time we portray the Father's heart to someone. I could keep going, but then this book would never be published. Let us just say the reason gemstones are so valuable is because they represent the love of the Father's heart.

The Father's Heart

STONES OF FIRE, THE FATHER'S HEART

CHAPTER EIGHT

You win the bet –
You get your Pets

>─┼─<>─Ⓞ─<>─┼─<

Our God is so good to us and because He loves us (no other reason) He allows our pets to go to Heaven when they pass. To be sure I could share this with confidence; He has taken me to Heaven and shown me several individuals' pets waiting for them in Heaven, including my own dog! Below are those stories.

<u>CHESTER</u>

This wonderful story takes place in 2008, when Bradford, 8 years old at the time, found out what God had prepared for his pet goldfish, Chester, in order to care for him in Heaven until Bradford would eventually arrive himself!

That particular day, I had stopped by the dance studio where my daughters both worked and took class. I had dropped something off, and got into a conversation about Heaven with one of the mothers (this was normal). This time it was with Paula and her son Bradford who was there too. We began to discuss about whether pets go to Heaven or not and Bradford got very excited when I said, "Yes, they certainly do, because you love them, God takes them"! Paula started to tell me about Bradford's goldfish, Chester, he had as a little boy and how when it died they gave him a farewell service. When she said, "You better tell him good-bye because you will never see him again", Bradford passionately responded, "No, Mama, I will see him again, in Heaven". She told him again that pets do not have souls so they do not go to Heaven! Well, Bradford would have none of that and he said, "I know God took my fish to Heaven". As they were talking amongst themselves, suddenly I was no longer aware of my surroundings and was taken again by the Spirit of God and shown Bradford's mansion that was still under construction in Heaven.

It looked like a castle with towers and everything, but still had many areas that were not completed.

The back portion of his mansion was finished and so I was shown that portion. It blessed me to see that Chester (all cute and orange) was indeed there and God had created an aquarium waterway that went through Bradford's entire mansion, even up the sides of doorways and down the other side.

In each room there was a 'bowl' that came out from the waterway, so that Chester could prop himself up on his fins and visit with Bradford. It then continued along every wall until it ended in the 'pool room' where there was a waterfall slide going into a swimming pool. I heard the Lord say, "Chester is excited, because when Bradford gets home, they will be able to swim together in the pool". Wow, I thought that was so cool and I was sure Bradford would love it too!

A few moments later I was back in the room but they were unaware I had ever left, until I told them what I saw. Bradford was so excited and his mom just stood there in shock and then she said. "That is exactly what Bradford had said to her before they arrived at the studio. He had insisted again that Bradford was in Heaven and then said, "Not only is he there, but when I get there, we will swim together in a pool"! How exciting that God showed me that to confirm to Bradford that he was right!

It also confirms that if he cares about a simple goldfish named Chester, I know he cares about all of our precious pets. I hope you enjoy the sketch of Chester waiting in Bradford's mansion; where one day they will swim together! Praise God for His goodness!

Statement by Bradford, November 12, 2010

When Mrs. Kat told me that she had just seen my mansion in heaven; I was really excited! At that moment I wanted God to take me to see Chester, but I knew I had more to do here and I'm so glad God cares.

Statement by Paula Willis, November 12, 2010

When my son and I were talking with Kat at the dance studio that day, she started to share about pets being in heaven. I thought to myself that God had sent her to confirm this about Chester, Bradford's fish, that was very special to him. It was amazing to see that even though Chester was a small goldfish, he used to react every time Bradford would come to his fish bowl; sometimes my son even patted him. Bradford is an animal lover and a natural with any kind of animal.

When Kat was sharing her book with us, I told her about Chester, and how much that fish meant to Bradford. In the little ceremony we did in our back yard after he died, I tried to comfort my son. I looked at him and my heart couldn't believe the words that came out of his mouth with such powerful meaning. I will never forget that day when I said to him, "Bradford it is time to say goodbye to Chester as you will never see him again." He looked at me and said, "No, Mama, I will see him again in heaven." I was broken because he was so sure of what he was saying. I had to tell him, "Bradford, fish do not have souls, which they need to go to heaven." He ignored my statement and said, "Chester WILL be in heaven."

While we were sharing this story amongst my family, Kat stopped us and began to tell us that the Lord had just shown her Bradford's mansion in heaven and that Chester would be there waiting for him. He got so excited and started to jump up and down. It was an incredible moment as she shared how the wall had a 'waterway' that the fish could swim in and follow Bradford in every room. She also told him that not only would he be able to talk to Chester, but swim too; because the mansion had an indoor pool with a waterfall slide where they could swim together.

My daughter and I looked at each other and started telling Kat, earlier that day we were talking about heaven during our home schooling and Bradford had said how cool it would be if his mansion had a swimming pool and slide so that he could swim with Chester. In his mind he always believed that Chester would be there in heaven but after that day with Kat, he had absolute confirmation of this and also God's goodness to our lives. Bradford is now 11 years old and Chester is still part of his life. Every night he thanks God that Chester will be there waiting for him. Everyone that knows Bradford, knows how special Chester is to him. I am so grateful that God showed Kat about Chester living in Heaven, because if he is there, so are all pets!

SALLY

This story is about a pet we bought for my father when he turned 60 and was living on a small farm. Her name was Sally and she was the cutest pig you ever saw. Pigs are considered one of the smartest mammals God created and Sally proved that many times over. She only weighted about 6 lbs at the time she was given; but by the time she departed for Heaven, she weighed a hefty 1,100 lbs. Now this pig was never going to be raised for someone's BBQ and I think she knew that. Her life was not too bad, her pen included a shower which she turned on and off as she pleased and a warm stall to lie in when it was cold. Every day my dad would go out and talk to her about the things of God and the pig really enjoyed those conversations. My dad just had to preach to somebody and Sally was a captive audience. The day Sally died, she pushed the heavy wall of her pen over, went around to the front of the house, laid under a tree and went to Heaven. My dad found her, got a backhoe and buried her on the back acreage of his farm. They had a short service to say good-by and even though my dad would miss his 'listening buddy', he knew she would be waiting for him in

Heaven. That big pig had given my dad a lot of joy with her life. I know animals cannot be 'saved', but I do know that God takes your pets to Heaven because we love them.

One of the few times I was permitted to see my father in Heaven (he never knew I was present) was to show me where our pets were being cared for until our eventual arrival in Heaven. I saw my father walking across his ranch property and following behind him was Sally the pig (with two mice riding on her back). Behind her, was a continual line of pets I recognized from my youth including my brother Joey's duck, Max; my brother RJ's alligator, Charlie; my cat, Little Bit; my brother Ray's iguana, Iggie, and so many others, as well as ones who had recently arrived. Since I am one of fifteen, you can imagine how long that line was. My dad was very generous about us having them; and although we did not have many things the world would call valuable, we loved our pets. They would include many dogs, cats, birds, turtles, hamsters, snakes (including the one with a glass eye); but also pigs, owls, alligators, mice, iguanas, ducks, pigeons, a bat and many frogs, toads and assorted big bugs! We even came up with a plan that would have worked to bring world peace;

we figured since we were able to get the cats and pigeons to eat out of the same dish without eating each other, it had to work on humans! Any of us could have presided over a funeral as we had lots of practice burying the pets. We loved them all and made sure they had a proper send-off to Heaven.

Just know that God has made sure you will have the pets you loved in eternity. It also happens to be one of the most asked questions I receive, Do your pets go to Heaven? The answer is yes!

MOLLY

Just because I am the author and I loved her, I want to share the story of Molly, my own yorkie who shared our lives for sixteen years. She was so cute when she came into our lives and made us laugh when she would actually smile at people. This was one smart dog and we knew somehow, she could tell time. Every day at 11:00 am she would go and wait under the mail slot at the front door. That was when the mailman would come and she was ready for action. When the mail was put through the slot, she would snatch it up and run all over the house with it. We were thankful that somehow she only shredded the junk mail and not the other which was important. Life went on and all of us loved her dearly and we were grateful she let us live in 'her' house with her.

As the years went by, Molly started to age and actually died several times, but I prayed and brought her back. It did teach me an important lesson, when it is time to let them go, we should not try to keep them here. The last time she almost died, I should have let her go, but I called her back and this caused her to have no quality of life; she could not see or hear very well. I had to go to Prayer Mountain late in May and had a call from my Mom saying that she believed Molly would not last until I returned. This time I only asked the Father to keep her until I could return home to tell her I loved her and say goodbye.

God was faithful and when I walked in at 2:00am she was still here. I bent over picked her up and after holding her for several hours and telling her how blessed her little life had made me and that I was sorry I had kept her beyond her allotted time; I released her to Heaven. About an hour later she was carried to Heaven by my guardian angel (they always carry your pets to Heaven) and taken to my father's ranch to await my home going!

Now I know some of you think all this is silly, but I promise, it is blessing many pet lovers. About two hours after her passing, the father decided to give me a gift by allowing me to see Molly in Heaven. I saw her racing down the streets of gold with several pieces of mail in her mouth and I knew Heaven did not have a mail system. Then he let me see what she was chasing; in front of Molly was a huge angel dressed in a postman's uniform and every now and then he would drop letters from his pouch. I was laughing at the strange site and then was shown there was another hundred or so dogs, chasing the same angel! How precious that he even cared about the very thing that Molly enjoyed doing. Don't be concerned about your pets in heaven; I am certain they have as good a time as everyone else that lives there!

CHESTER

CHAPTER NINE

Fun from the Son: Surf Park and Remember When Gallery

⊱⊰⊹⊱⊙⊰⊹⊱⊰

Yes, Heaven is fun and it is part of my commission to make that clear. Heaven is holy, but it is FUN too. You cannot get any more holy after you get there; there will be no classes on that subject. When you accepted Christ as your savior, His 'holy' blood sacrifice gave you entrance into Heaven and nothing else. We (being pure) will be 'like' Him when we see Him, in other words; we will be as sanctified and righteous as we can possibly get.

Even the Word says you must be like a LITTLE CHILD to enter into the Kingdom of Heaven and part of that is because they like to have fun. Believe me; if you are expecting it to be like a monastery you are mistaken. If we are to be like little kids the last thing the Father would do is make Heaven like a monastery because I know exactly what a 5 or 8 year old would do in such a place. They would be running through the hallways, laughing, singing and being very loud with their friends. That is why our (young hearted) Father in Heaven said, "You prayed to Me as a family on earth, now we will play as a family in Heaven!"

Wow, who would have ever guessed that Heaven actually cares whether you have fun places to go to? Well, I assure you that you will never be bored in that supernatural place! I will do my best to describe several of those places.

The Surf Park

Once I was caught up and shown this amazing place created near the base of a huge mountain; it was an enormous surf park called "Wipeout". The 75 foot waves were generated when the water coming off the top of this mountain (several hundred feet high) crashed down into the blue green lagoon and surged forward, racing toward the beach. This water is still a part of the Crystal Sea, so you can imagine how exquisite the foam on the waves is! Every surfer or lover of the ocean will be so excited when they see that the Father did not forget them. Can you imagine getting to surf every wave, every time? Of course, that does not mean you become expert after the first time because Heaven has a way of 'surprising' you that will challenge to go beyond your normal limits!

There were other things to enjoy at this park and as usual, some were supernatural. Many types of whales and other animals were there that allowed us to interact like we never could on earth. You really experience the same friendship Adam had with the animals and creatures God placed in the Garden of Eden.

Remember When Gallery

This place will be enjoyed by everybody who ever lives in Heaven; as everyone's life has been recorded for their enjoyment when they arrive there. There will be no sin, no tragedy or sad events in these mini movies; only the fun filled, hilarious things we did while growing up. Also, any significant or rewarding moment in your life that was special to you. It is a wonderful thing to invite family members, friends and even new acquaintances to go to the Remember

When Gallery and sit in your own private theater and view your life. You may think that nothing ever happened that would fit in any of those categories but the Father assures me, you just don't remember everything!

I personally will enjoy viewing my mother's growing up years as I am certain she left out the unbelievable things. She was 'miss propriety' teaching us the 'proper' things to do and say and yet I heard from a reliable source that she and her brother actually ran through part of the sewer system in New York (not the city) in the 1940's (of course, it was the 'clean' part of the sewer). It should also make a good showing when I view my brother around age 11 (not RJ) jumping his bicycle over the canal (like Evil Knievel) at the end of our street and embedding it half way down in the wall; the firemen had to rescue him! Having 15 siblings could take some time sharing all the funny things they did, but don't worry, my Mother is writing a book all about it! That should give you a good example of what I mean about everyone enjoying this place.

There are many other enjoyable places in Heaven, some of them I mention in Volume I such as the Amusement park, Hall of the Nations and of course, the Reality Theaters. Some people may have a problem embracing the fact that Heaven is fun, but if they end up there (and I pray they do) they will find out for themselves.

The Surf Park

CHAPTER TEN

Portal Visits – Close-up

><>+O+<><

Once again, the Holy Spirit took me to this wonderful place where Heaven comes to watch those on the earth (Hebrews 12:1). This time, I was sent to observe a family of four; a father, mother and two of their children watching their loved one receive Christ as savior. The whole family had been killed in an auto accident, except their older son, whom they had prayed for while on earth and then declared the will of God over his life after arriving in Heaven. I will never forget the look on their faces, such joy and victory. Because they would not give up on him, God did not give up on him. I wanted to include this illustration to let you know your loved ones do not forget you after they depart to Heaven.

It is so important to make a stand for your family members' salvation and once you do this, please do not start speaking badly about them. You cannot become double-minded, as that will cancel your prayers. Instead, you can say what they declare over loved ones from Heaven! "We declare you will become a Mighty Man (Woman) of God, We declare you will not miss your Destiny, and We declare you will become a living testimony of the saving power of Jesus Christ". When you say things like that, you will be releasing power on behalf of your loved ones salvation instead of confirming what satan has planned for them; your words become weapons against the enemy!

People are allowed to see many things concerning their families on earth and no significant event is ever missed! We serve an amazing God who desires that all come to the saving knowledge of Jesus Christ!

Portal Visit

PORTAL VISIT UP CLOSE

CHAPTER ELEVEN

Suicide – the Truth

>─┼─◆>─┼─◦─┼<◆─┼─<

The Father was quite clear that there would be a chapter to answer questions we have all had concerning this subject: Do those who commit suicide go to Hell or do some go to Heaven? The Holy Spirit gave me the answer, and as always it was so simple, most of us missed it!

The world's definition of suicide is: The act or instance of <u>intentionally</u> killing oneself. The psychiatrists explain that once despair (hopelessness) sets in, there is almost no way to turn one from it. Sometimes there is a note left explaining why, but many times there is little or no warning. Many do it out of spite or hate against another, to purposely bring them suffering to punish them. Then some, like the terrorists, think of it as an honor to sacrifice themselves in order to kill others whom they or their cause want to wipe out.

There is one more viewpoint no one mentions and that is the Father's opinion! Here is the explanation I was given. God looks at each case separately and if the person ending their life is a Believer, He does not always call it suicide. If the person had lost control of their normal reasoning; either because of physical, emotional or mental trauma; then he calls it 'ending their suffering', not committing suicide. In other words, all those individuals would go to Heaven!

I was shown three different individuals in Heaven who had 'ended their suffering'. They were from three different ages and although I cannot reveal their names I will disclose a little about their situations that preceded their leaving this world. One was a thirteen years old boy who had lived his whole life in very abusive foster homes. He did receive Christ before passing, but continued to have night terrors of the things he experienced. In his last year of life, he did manage to get placed in a Christian home as did his younger brother. They loved him and prayed for him, but he did not ever recover from the mental and emotional torture he had experienced. Finally, he could not cope any longer and he ended his suffering. When I was taken to Heaven and viewed his life it was like seeing a different person. He was filled with the life and love of God and he was playing in a rock band and another time I saw him playing on a junior football team. When I returned and shared with his friends, they were overjoyed as these were the two things he always wanted to do.

The other person was in their 20's and, although a longtime Believer, had been in a serious auto accident and was on very strong medication. The medication had severe side effects and took away any normal reasoning he once had. It was not long before he ended the agony and, of course, was taken to Heaven. I viewed him several times and knew he was very sorry for causing pain to his family and cried out to the Lord to let them know he had gone to Heaven and not hell. His family, also Believers, had been told by many (unfortunately from the religious group) that he had gone to hell! It changed their lives when I revealed what the Father had allowed me to observe him doing in Heaven. He was in his father's amazing mountain home and enjoying many of the things they always did together. The thing I will never forget was what I saw on the mantel, a trophy with these words:

God   1
Satan   0

This by no means gives anyone the right to end their lives, you could never be sure what the Father's decision would be concerning you. Most everyone I saw who had ended their suffering had NO control over their mind or emotions. You can be free from depression and suicidal thoughts (which are sent by evil spirits), through the power of the blood of Jesus.

If you still have your own reasoning and you have accepted Christ, go before the throne in prayer and say, "Because I am a child of God, as an act of my will, I chose to be free and satan has NO hold on me"! Get rid of anything in your house that promotes satan's kingdom, such as witchcraft in any form and if you have ever been to a séance, had your palm read or played with any occult games that contact the dead or that imply to tell the future; you need to repent and renounce any association with those things. Other things that give the enemy entrance into your life are demonic trading cards, the obsessive games of Extreme Violence – becoming a virtual player in the game, vampire movies/products (this is a spirit of death) and any pornographic materials! After repenting for watching, reading or owning any of those items, pray and break the power of the enemy off you and your home. People need to make the right choices in their lives, because as the Holy Spirit revealed to me, "whatever you enter into, will enter into you".

We must choose Life and not things related to Death and then live your life like you actually believe Heaven is watching. If you could see your guardian angel with you all the time, you would choose more carefully. Guard your heart and put the things of God there instead of the things of this world. You can have as much of God in your life as you want, it requires a 'surrender' many are not willing to give. It also requires meditating on the Word of God so that your mind is renewed.

I would also encourage you to play anointed worship in your home all the time, even while you sleep. It does not need to be loud or in a place that it would offend others in your home; but play it somewhere. If you do not know what type of music I am talking about, here are some people that literally 'draw' the presence of God; Joann McFatter, Jason Upton, Jake Hamilton or Phil Wickham, Kathryn Marquis and of course, Leeland. If you like a more 'radical' sound (definitely for the younger crowd) try Kelanie Gloeckler, John Mark McMillan or Rick Pino, and any of their music will create an atmosphere that Heaven will want to come and inhabit! The enemy hates it when you worship God as he feels all worship should go to him. When you are experiencing your worst days, PLEASE praise God! It is the most powerful warfare you can do!

CHAPTER TWELVE

The Place of Angels

➤┤◆➤◦◆┤◄

One of the most exciting places I was taken to is the Headquarters of the Host – Heaven's armies, which are under the command of Michael, one of the Archangels! His powerful face although beautiful, is one of a focused, fierce leader! If asked, Michael would tell you His most treasured moment was when he was allowed to 'boot' Lucifer out of Heaven.

The best way I can describe this 'place of power' in Heaven is that it looks like the largest, most amazing castle I had ever seen. It was hundreds of feet high, filled with the Glory of God and disappeared right into the sky; almost becoming a part of it. There are HUGE angels in Heaven, some the size of our planet. Clouds of mystical smoke surround this place of Heaven's armies.

Although one of the most important places there, not many people have toured it. Mostly, because of the intense activity and the fact that their headquarters are in a far country, even the ends of Heaven (as stated in Isaiah 13:3). Let me just say, no one would ever fear for their safety if they saw some of the warring angels and especially those they call the 'transforming angels' whose bodies appear to be made from some type of metal alloy. They literally transform into a 'ship' and streak across the universe to wherever the 'heat' of the battle is and they do not have to carry weapons; they 'are' the weapon which is powerfully used against Satan's armies! They don't have two eyes in their head like humans, but have a wide band that surrounds their head, filled with eyes, the enemy cannot evade them.

There is no way I could keep track of all the types of angels I have seen; but will share a few with you. Another group I have observed are the Courier and Scribe angels; both directed by Gabriel, another of the Archangels. These angels do not usually fight, but most do carry some type of weapon, especially if they are escorting any of the Believers to Heaven. One of the jobs of Scribe angels is to deliver messages to individuals on earth and/or collect (record) them too. The Courier angels are usually present in meetings collecting the prayers and worship of the people. They arrive on a stairway from Heaven, carrying these large purple vials and they 'scoop' up the prayers and praise and then go back to the throne room and empty them into the golden bowls before the altar of God! It is considered incense in Heaven and the aroma of our worship releases a sweet smell before the throne of God! At the end of this chapter, you will see an illustration of some courier angels collecting the worship on the National Day of Prayer in my city! Hundreds poured in and began 'swooping' down in front of the people to catch their words as they stood praying for our nation. It was a beautiful site and I was blessed that the Father allowed me to 'see' into the spirit realm and capture it for all to enjoy!

Many other types of angelic and created beings exist in Heaven; such as the Cherubim with eyes in their bodies and six wings. They stand at the four corners of the Throne (mentioned in Revelations 4) as they declare HOLY, HOLY, HOLY the room begins to shake from the power and authority in their words. Besides the four in the throne room, there are others that God sends over the earth to 'see' what is going on. They are the 'eyes that go to and fro in the earth' and are continually searching the hearts of men!

Many do not look anything like what we are used to seeing in the artwork produced on earth. There are some that have facets in their faces and have blue fire coming from their heads and these are able to compress themselves as thin as a sheet of paper and pass over a congregation to release fire from Heaven. If you are ever in a service where one comes, you will be eternally changed by the passion he releases!

Some angels have a masculine appearance, but I have seen a few with a beautiful feminine look to them and these are protectors and caretakers of the waterfalls and brooks you will enjoy all over the heavenly realm. When they speak, you are captivated by the beauty of their words and the music that is carried in those words. Their appearance is that of a green mist with thousands of lights sparkling within. Our God is such an amazing creator and it makes touring Heaven one continuous adventure after another!

Angels Collecting Worship

CHAPTER THIRTEEN

Sports in the Extreme –
No helmets required

>–⟨⟩–◦–⟨⟩–≺

I was definitely surprised by this revelation about Heaven, that sports are played there; but as worship! How can this possibly happen, it is really simple. There are always three scoreboards, one for each team and then above them, one for Jesus. Jesus gets all points, but the competition between teams is even more aggressive because each team wants to make more points for Him! The winning team gets to carry Jesus across the court or field and celebrate with him after the event. The other thing that makes it different is that no one ever gets injured, no matter what the sport! There is never a need for protective equipment which means the athlete will have more flexibility for movement or speed.

The reason sports are there is because everyone uses their gifts to bless one another and athletes have gifts! I don't think that will happen in hell though, so they better be sure they know where they will be spending eternity!

I have seen golf tournaments, football games, basketball, fishing, all water sports, barrel racing with horses and many of the extreme sports. It is certain that all sports that do not require abusive contact (such as boxing) exist in Heaven! Sports enthusiast will be excited to find the Father did not forget those who have athletic gifts.

CHAPTER FOURTEEN

Hall of the Super Hero's – God's Generals & Intercessors

>–‹+›•⊖•‹+›–‹

This is another amazing place God created to honor those who stand in the gap for others. The sign, floating above the building, read – Hall of Super Heroes! One of the highest callings is that of an intercessor and when you visit this place you are able to actually view these mighty men and women of God as they prayed in the past.

You enter this place that glows with the Glory of God and pass down long corridors where you will see the faces of intercessors (who now live in Heaven) engraved right into the wall. As you stand gazing at them, light begins to form around the outside of the engraved face and suddenly, you are pulled back into the time of that particular prayer warrior.

As you stand there watching these mighty warriors crying out to God on behalf of others, you realize that the Throne of God was right there in front of them the minute they said, "Father"! When they began to pray, you would see a spiritual 'sword' begin to form from their words and the angel of the Lord standing and waiting for them to finish. As they finished, the angel would grab the weapon that their words had just created and go and fight the enemy concerning what they had prayed. This was an immediate reaction and it happens anytime a Believer is fervently and effectually praying (James 5:16).

This revelation should definitely have an effect on everyone's prayer life. You DO make a difference with your focused prayers and according to the book of Daniel, angels do come for your words. They become weapons in the hand of your God and do harm against the enemy's plans; so keep praying and declaring God's Word over yourself, your family and others.

CHAPTER FIFTEEN

God's Timeline – Heaven Invasion

The Father wants you to know this is NOT the time to be hoarding food, hiding your money and walking in fear! He does not have plans to go bankrupt in Heaven, nor is he concerned about the grim predictions of man. Instead, He is laughing at the enemy's and mans' plans for this earth! If He is in control of your life, He is your provider and protector. It is not time for the end to come because there is something that must be fulfilled first – the saints anointing, Joel 2. Even if there are wars and even some disasters, it will not prevent God from coming and showing up and showing off in His people!

During one of my many visits to the throne room, I was shown a fascinating thing called 'God's Timeline' which was embedded right into the floor. You could walk up and look down at 'eternity' and see from the beginning, Genesis 1:1 (creation of the heavens & earth) to the end of time & space, Revelation 22 (creation of the new earth). There was a 'mark' in the Timeline every time God planned to intervene (with an action/divine event) in the earth. I was told that these 'interventions' occurred whenever a 'fullness of time' had come to completion. For instance, a fullness of time had come when Adam and Eve were created, when Christ was born, another when He began His ministry, and other times, the Upper Room experience, Azusa Street Revival and so forth. These were all 'divine events' on the Timeline and since they are God's; nothing or no one can prevent them from happening! We are so close to another of those events taking place on earth; the inscription by the mark read, "Heaven Invasion/Joel 2".

This subject is the most talked about thing in Heaven – The Invasion of earth. On earth it is also called the Great Awakening, the former & latter rain, the Restoration of all things, the Greater works, and last great move of God. Because this is a divine event, no demon, neither man, nor government can stop it from coming forth! Millions of healing angels are being trained to help empty the Body Parts Warehouse during this move of God that will usher in the Harvest of souls during this season.

The Father gave me open visions of what must take place during this Holy season on earth! In Heaven they call it a 'habitation' not just a 'visitation' of God's spirit. The Father will send His Spirit with tidal waves of God's love into the heart of every person; Joel 2 (all flesh). The Believers will start loving one another and pastors from different denominations will begin to trust one another. Many Christians will begin to perform amazing miracles the earth has never experienced before.

God will even allow His angels to be photographed and taped; shown on TV, the internet, magazines and newspapers! People will demand that the media show these divine encounters and miracles as they will be occurring everywhere. I was shown that during this movement a Believer could walk through a hospital (not even touching the door knobs of rooms) and because of the Glory they carry, every sick person will be healed.

Another thing I was shown was the authority of the Believer become very powerful as they receive an understanding of who they are in Christ. As they walk in holiness, learn to release the anointing that abides in every Believer (I John 2:27), step out and take authority over satan and his devils, I saw evil flee like dust from whole cities. The habitation of Glory will be so evident in some regions that I saw people taking their dead in cars to those regions and when they crossed the state lines, the dead came back to life.

The Word says in Joel 2 that even children will prophesy during this time. So stand up and declare what God meant when He said, "Let us (the Godhead) make man in our image and after our likeness". This meant their outside image (body) and also their inside image (spirit). The Word says we are the temple of the Holy Spirit and the fullness of the Godhead bodily; so we need to start living like we believe it! Get your lives in order and cleanse yourself through repentance. There is no evil, fear, sickness, stress, indecency or depression in God's image; so there should be none in ours! Start speaking positive words that bring 'life' to yourself and others; things that God says and not what man says. Live according to guidelines God sets and not the world. You should not have a problem understanding what that means, as Jesus said to pray, "God's will be done on earth as it is in Heaven" (not as it is done in the world)!

Don't you know that your guardian angel goes everywhere with you and will not leave you, even when they have to go places that belong to satan and watch things your eyes should never see. Your angel will cover his eyes with his wings until you leave those places. If you make it to Heaven you will find out every time they saved your life, even when you fought against the things of God in your life. Be Holy even as He is Holy if you want to do great things during this time on earth.

CHAPTER SIXTEEN

FUEL FROM HEAVEN – GRACE

>─┼─◆─○─◆─┼─<

Even though you have read amazing things about Heaven and what Heaven is about to do on this earth, you will probably benefit more from this one little chapter than all the previous! It is how to walk in Abundant Grace from the Father. Please take it seriously if you want your life to change starting tomorrow morning. It will cost you nothing if you try it, so I challenge you! If you try it for one week, it will be one of the best weeks of your life! You will walk in peace, joy and blessing and it is freely given to you!

Several years ago the Father did me one of the greatest favors ever; He himself taught me about asking for Abundant Grace. You know, that 'Grace for help in time of need' that the Word talks about getting when you go before the Throne of Grace in

Heaven? Well, the Father took me there one morning and told me, "I am going to do something that will bless everyone in your life; I am going to teach you about Abundant Grace.

Every morning you get up and come out of your room, and everyone sees you and hears you, your thoughts, your attitudes, your selfish opinions. So I have decided to have mercy on them and teach you something that will change you starting tomorrow morning! It is the grace I filled my Son with while He was yet a child. It is one of the things that helped carry Him through all the days of His life! So, every day before you get out of bed, if you will look up to Heaven and say, <u>Father, I ask for and receive Grace for this day, Amen!</u> We will download from Heaven, 'fuel' for that day; we are the only ones who know everything you will face each day. It does not mean you won't face trials anymore, it means no matter what it is, it will not be able to touch you; as you now are filled with abundant grace from Me for that day. It will cause you to be victorious and if you can teach your family to do the same, you will all walk and live in harmony with each other. I freely offer it, but you must ask for it"!

I did start asking every morning and I felt like a new person and even if everyone else I met throughout the day, had a 'bad' day, I did not! Wow, it was hard to believe my life could be so different just by inviting Heaven to give me 'fuel' for every day and yes, my family definitely noticed a difference in me. After teaching this to all who lived in my house, we all walk in that grace, peace and joy – NO MORE STRIFE. It is not hard to tell if someone did not ask, they stuck out like a sore thumb, showing up with attitudes, opinions and their old self! We will turn and say, "Go ask for Grace", and once they do, they change! I would challenge everyone to ask for grace everyday and see if it does not change the way you walk through life. It will bring VICTORY! You have not, because you ask not!

CHAPTER SEVENTEEN

The Father's Love Letter

****
****

➤⊱◦⟡◦⊰➤

This beautiful blending of the Holy Scriptures
is used with permission
from Father Heart Communication.

My Child...

You may not know me, but I know everything about you...Psalm 139:1 I know when you sit down and when you rise up...Psalm 139:2 I am familiar with all your ways...Psalm 139:3 Even the very hairs on your head are numbered...Matthew 10:29-31 For you were made in my image...Genesis 1:27 In me you live and move and have your being...Acts 17:28 For you are my offspring...Acts 17:28 I knew you even before you were conceived...Jeremiah 1:4-5 I chose you when I planned creation...Ephesians 1:11-12 You were not a mistake, for all your days are written in my book ...Psalm 139:15-16 I determined the exact time of your birth and where you would live...Acts 17:26 You are fearfully and wonderfully made...Psalm 139:14 I knit you together in your mother's womb...Psalm 139:13 And brought you forth on the day you were born... Psalm 71:6 I have been misrepresented by those who don't know me...John 8:41-44 I am not distant and angry, but am the complete expression of love...1 John 4:16 And it is my desire to lavish my love on you... 1John 3:1 Simply because you are my child and I am your Father... 1John 3:1 I offer you more than your earthly father ever could... Matthew 7:11 For I am the perfect Father...Matthew 5:48 Every good gift that you receive comes from my hand... James 1:17 For I am your provider and I meet all your needs...Matthew 6:31-33 My plan for your future has always been filled with hope...Jeremiah 29:11 Because I love you with an everlasting love...Jeremiah 31:3 My thoughts toward you are countless as the sand on the seashore... Psalm 139:17-18 And I rejoice over you with singing...Zephaniah 3:17 I will never stop doing good to you...Jeremiah 32:40 For you are my treasured possession...Exodus 19:5 I desire to establish you with all my heart and all my soul...Jeremiah 32:41 And I want to show you great and marvelous things...Jeremiah 33:3 If you seek me with all your heart, you will find me...Deuteronomy 4:29 Delight in me and I will give you the desires of your heart...Psalm 37:4 For it is I who gave you those desires...Philippians 2:13 I am able to do more for you than you could possibly imagine... Ephesians 3:20 For I am your greatest encourager...2 Thessalonians 2:16-17 I am also the Father who comforts you in all your troubles...2Corinthians 1:3-4 When you are brokenhearted, I am close to you...Psalm 34:18 As a shepherd carries a lamb, I have carried you close to my heart...Isaiah 40:11 One day I will wipe away every tear from your eyes...Revelation 21:3-4 And I'll take away all the pain you have suffered on this earth... Revelation 21:3-4 I am your Father, and I love you even as I love my son, Jesus...John 17:23 For in Jesus, my love for you is revealed...John 17:26 He is the exact representation of my being...Hebrews 1:3 He came to demonstrate that I am for you, not against you...Romans 8:31 And to tell you that I am not counting your sins...2 Corinthians 5:18-19 Jesus died so that you and I could be reconciled ...2Corinthians 5:18-19 His death was the ultimate expression of my love for you...1 John 4:10 I gave up everything I loved that I might gain your love...

Romans 8:31-32 If you receive the gift of my son Jesus, you receive me...1 John 2:23 And nothing will ever separate you from my love again ... Romans 8:38-39 Come home and I'll throw the biggest party heaven has ever seen ... Luke 15:7 I have always been Father, and will always be Father...Ephesians 3:14-15 My question is... Will you be my child?... John 1:12-13 I am waiting for you....... Luke 15:11-32

...Love, Your Dad

Almighty God

Father Heart Communications

Copyright 1999 www.FathersLoveLetter.com www. FatherLovesJacksonville.com For Products & Ministry of Father's Love, Contact Ambassadors Bill and Deborah Fisher (904) 249-3368 www. HotPursuitMinistries.com

APPENDIX

Questions and Answers

About One Quest International

About the Author

About the Illustrator

Standing with Israel – God's Chosen

Prophecies

Products Catalog

Suggested reading

Notes

Prayer List

55 QUESTIONS WITH ANSWERS

Surveyed 400 people from different age groups ranging from age 5 to 95, ethnic groups and different states with the same question:

"If you could ask God one question about Heaven, what would it be?"

Ken, Age 73 — Edgewater, CO
Is the 2nd heaven also a planet?

No, it is the domain of Satan and it takes up the space between earth's atmosphere and the Third Heaven, where God lives.

Dosano, Age 12 — Golden, CO
Do we have amazing abilities (in heaven)?

Yes, because you are now living in a supernatural realm. You can run faster, jump higher and even

fly (without wings) over certain areas of Heaven.
Many things like opening doors, traveling and even
talking are done with your thoughts. You will still
use your mouth to speak and sing with but you def-
initely communicate with your mind if you want to.

Sam, Age 28 — Golden, CO
If everything on earth now is a glimpse of heaven
and if everything on earth was first an idea that
came from heaven, does that mean Adam and Eve
learned to drive a car and fly planes once they went
to heaven?

They have certainly adapted to Heaven's intelli-
gence level and way of living, but you don't have to
just drive a car (you can fly them too) oR fly an ordi-
nary plane (you get a star cruiser that uses light
as fuel) as they also have space buses, transport
kiosks (where you travel from one side of Heaven to
another on beams of light.

Kiel, Age 32 — Ackerman, MS
Will there be a place we can sit on the porch and
smell the rain (storm) coming? (Since it doesn't rain)

You would probably like to live near the Valley of the
Falls, where it always smells like fresh rain. This is

caused from the mist created by the 50 waterfalls in that valley. Anyone who goes to Heaven can have a wrap-around-porch to relax on with their friends. By the way, they do have a place in Heaven just like the rain forest on earth and it does rain there!

Cody, Age 10 – state unknown
Is there a temperature in heaven?

You never really notice that, since your 'spirit being' is not affected the same way by heat or cold. There are places in Heaven where you can be in the snow and it does feel cool but in a fun way!

Shane, Age 13 – State unknown
In Revelations they speak of strange animals. Do they have a special name?

They are not animals, but very intelligent created beings that walk upright like people and they are called Living Creatures. Read Revelations 4 for more information.

Glory, Age 8 — Genessee, CO
Does heaven have a beauty salon?

Yes, it is very different than the ones on the earth, as they use no chemicals to curl or color your hair. It is done by light and only takes seconds.

Sergio, Age 75 — Canada
What would be the earth age?

I do not know exact age, but I know it is millions of years old.

Leisa, Age Unknown — Pontotoc, MS
Will we be allowed individual alone time with Jesus?

Yes, he loves to spend alone time with everyone as we are all special to him.

Sarah, Age 13 — Ponte Vedra Beach, FL
Why did you make people?

Because God wanted to have a family.

Dorian, Age 9 — Unknown
Do you give all people a second chance?

God gives everyone many chances to repent and belong to Him; they actually get all their life up until the day they die!

Mrs. Riley, Age 65 — Okalona, MS
Will we be able to wear jewelry in heaven?

When we depart from this world and go to Heaven, we will use our gifts and talents to bless everyone living there. So that means if someone was a jeweler on this earth, they will always be a jeweler; even in Heaven. Yes, you get amazing jewelry to wear and it is FREE!

Dakota, Age 15 — state unknown
Will heaven still be there after the rapture takes place?

The bible says after we are raptured, we (the Believers who accepted Jesus) will be in Heaven celebrating the Marriage Supper of the Lamb, so it will definitely be there!

Maya, Age 12 — Jacksonville, FL
How did God determine to make all of this stuff in heaven?

He created things that people will love to have or do when they get to Heaven. Everybody has a mansion made just the way they would like it too!

Christina, Age 19 — Jacksonville, FL
Can you sleep and walk on clouds?

You will never sleep, because no one ever gets tired. I know people float across the skies of Heaven when they worship, but have never seen someone walk on clouds.

Kate, Age Unknown — North Carolina
Do we get to explore the universe in heaven?

God made all of His creation (including outer space) for His people to enjoy. They even get to pass through it on the way home to Heaven when they die.

Matt, Age 21 — Pontotoc, MS
Will we be able to see my tattoo on my spiritual body in heaven?

No, none of us will keep anything that was put on our physical body; we are spirit beings when we pass from this life and things like that do not remain on the spirit. However, the Bible says God himself will put His mark on us when we get to Heaven

Daniel, Age 17 — Pontotoc, MS

Are there people on other planets and other earth's in the universe?

NO, there are no other life forms in the whole universe except us humans who were born into this earth. However, when we are living on the new earth, as mentioned in Revelation, we will be able to do things we never could do before; such as travel to other planets because God will allow fun and exciting things to be created on them for us to enjoy while visiting.

Cindy, Age 41

Evergreen, CO

If someone doesn't receive the Lord before they die, will He appear to them and give them an opportunity to accept Him and be with Him in eternity after they die (on the way)?

That is not specifically promised in the Bible, but your prayers do make a difference if you belong to God and you are praying in faith for family members to get saved. It would certainly allow more opportunities for someone to know God and receive

Christ that would not have been possible if people were not praying for them!

Bonnie, Age 55 — Aurora, CO
Will we sleep in heaven?

No, you never get tired, because your spirit being is eternal and never needs rest!

Lindsay, Age 22 — Evergreen, CO
How can someone receive the honor of being picked up by God in His own chariot, when they die? They have spent their lives loving God and others. Also, they obeyed when asked by God; they never hesitated, even when it sounded foolish.

You have answered your own question; it has everything to do with living a life of surrender to God and allowing Him to use you. That is exactly what happened to Oral Roberts when he passed away; he was picked up in the Lord's own chariot.

Alee, Age 14 — Conifer, CO
What do doctors/ bankers do in heaven?

Some doctors give all the little babies a pretend check-up as a form of playtime. I do not know what bankers do, as there is no money needed in Heaven.

Keiarra, Age 9 — Jacksonville, FL
God, do we wear the same clothes in heaven?

NO, you get a beautiful gown and a robe like a king or queen wears; and an amazing wardrobe of tunic pants & tops which are needed in order to enjoy many of the places God made for us there.

Randi, Age 26 — Jacksonville, FL
God, how do you feel about people that commit suicide what happens, where do they go?

Every case is judged separately because every situation is different. God says they do not put people in hell, if they are looking for a way to 'end' their suffering (and are not in control of their own mind) especially, if they are christians.

Daina, Age 24 — Bowie, MD
Do our names change? If so, when? Is it different for unnamed babies (unborn)? Do they gain a name from God or the name their parents would have chosen?

People will call you by your first name only. However, when you get to Heaven the Father gives you a new 'nickname' that only He calls you by.

Little babies, who arrive in Heaven with no name, are given a nickname by the angels. Parents can still name their baby living in Heaven, even years later.

Carolina, Age Unknown — North Carolina
Can I help people still living to make a difference or is reincarnation possible?

NO one is EVER reincarnated! You get one life and that is it; so definitely help others find out about the Truth!

Grace, Age 7 ½ — Kittredge, CO
What do animals do in heaven?

Pets play a lot and wait in your mansion for you to come to Heaven. Many animals roam free, enjoy the beauty of Heaven and sometimes interact with people by giving them rides or just keep them company.

Leroy, Age 13 — Jacksonville, FL
How does heaven become larger every day?

It is a HUGE planet and every time someone dies and goes to Heaven, God makes new things for them to enjoy.

Joseph, Age Unknown — Denver, CO
Will we meet strangers that we prayed for their salvation (and they got saved?)

Certainly, God makes sure you get to meet them and you find out what your prayers produced on their behalf.

Jason, Age 20
Toronto, Canada
Where do demons come from?

All the demons are the fallen angels that were kicked out of Heaven with Lucifer (who later became Satan). They have become so defiled that they no longer have their original state of beauty. Some of them are bound in chains as they did things not permitted by God and are being held for judgement!

Jaylin, Age 13
Will we be judged in heaven?

Believers only go before the Judgment Seat of Christ (that is not being judged for sins), for things they decided to do themselves instead of what God called them to do. Such as, if God wanted them to become a judge and they decided to be a preacher instead, there would be no reward for anything they did as that preacher (those efforts would be burned up). We must use the gifts He gave us while on earth, if you do not know what your destiny is, then love God and others as yourself and He will make sure you do not miss your destiny!

Pharaoh, Age 15 — Jacksonville, FL
What kind of job are we going to do when we first get in heaven?

We will all use the gifts (designers, baker, artist, florist, loving people, trashmen pick up treasure in Heaven, etc..) God gave us to bless one another. We have all things in common means we share (without cost) our gifts and talents, the thing we love doing most, with everyone!

Pat, Age 62 — Morrison, CO
Is new heaven and new earth after the millennial (reign)?

Yes, the bible is very plain about this. It will be fantastic and we will not remember former things (our sins, whatever made us fearful or sad) on earth, it says all things will be new.

Emma, Age 6 — Pontotoc, MS
If I want to see an ant up close, will God shrink me to its size?

Never saw that happen, but I don't know why He wouldn't do it for you. He loves to bless His children.

Abagael, Age 14 — Jacksonville, FL
Does everybody in heaven worship God all at the same time?

Yes, they do this a lot in the Throne Room and sometimes all of Heaven worships Him at the same time!

Richard, Age 15 — Jacksonville, FL
Where is heaven?

Above our earth is our atmosphere and outer space, beyond that is the 2nd heaven where Lucifer lives, and then above that is the 3rd Heaven – where God, Jesus, Holy Spirit, the angels and the Redeemed live.

Beverly, Age 70 — Edgewater, CO
Is the rainbow round around the throne?

The rainbow goes from the floor up over God's throne like an arch and then down the other side to the floor of the Throne Room.

Raheem, Age 15 — unknown
Would I have angel wings?

NO, you do not become an angel. Wings are for the angels who are created beings made to serve God. You can, however, fly over certain places in Heaven; such as the Amusement Park.

Dane, Age 46 — Mississippi
Are there cars (antique, racing, convertibles) in heaven?

Yes, I actually saw a car show with all makes and models being present. God is so good to make many things we will love and enjoy.

Ta'shaun, Age 8 — Jacksonville, FL
Does God eat the food we eat?

I do not know if God does, but Jesus definitely eats the food in Heaven. The food is made out of light and almost anything we like to eat here is made there but no weight gain or allergies!

Debra, Age 46 — Okolona, MS
Is time consistent in heaven, like hours, minutes, or does it change on occasions?

Time does not exist in Heaven, but there are certain events that take place and you always just know when to be at them.

Malcom, Age 16 — Jacksonville, FL
God, I want to spend time with you. Will I be able to do that? Sit back ask you about many things.

God has made a way for you to be alone with Him because He loves you!

Joseph, Age 11 — Jacksonville, FL
Will we be able to see different people's mansions and angels in heaven?

YES, there are millions of different styles, models and architectures, and you will enjoy touring them when you get there. Everyone welcomes you to see their mansions. You will be shocked to see how

many different angels are in Heaven and how some of them are as big as our planet!

Nancy, Age 71 — Mississippi
What about speaking in tongues- the effect for prayer in Heaven?

No one in Heaven needs prayer and you don't pray as much as declare God's will over people who are still on earth.

Marty, Age 69 — Evergreen, CO
Why are we alone in a mansion and not with other family members?

You are never alone, because everyone visits all the time or you are visiting them. Also, all your family members will live very close to your mansion. You have your own 'special' place made with all the things you love and everyone is different from one another and God wanted all to be happy. Trust me; NO ONE will ever be lonely in Heaven!

Briana, Age 12 — Jacksonville, FL
Why are there dinosaur parks in heaven?

It is the place God made for dinosaurs to live as they need a place to stay too. You may visit or even ride on them in Heaven.

Michelle, Age 36 — Oklahoma City, OK
Is there a different type of guardian angel assigned for people who are required to go into the dark places or if they respond differently?

Every guardian angel is assigned to a specific person and that angel would adapt to whatever your job was. God knows what kind of angel to send and they will be faithful to watch over their person.

Unknown — London, Canada
In heaven, are we able to see and/ or communicate with our family and friends down on earth?

In Hebrews 12:1 it says there are a great 'cloud of witnesses' that have passed on before us. That would include any of your family members or friends who now live in Heaven, God created places for them to go and see and hear you; it is called The Portal.

Victor, Age 57 — Vermont

Lots of people/souls are going to heaven. You say everyone gets a mansion, how much real estate comes with the mansion? Like, do the structures adjoin each other?

Every mansion that God creates does include a lot of property and that property will include many things that person loves doing. If you mean are their condos or townhomes, I never saw any. There are some mansions that have a 'common' area at the end of their mansion, where other family member's mansions adjoin to so that they can all have a space to enjoy things they did together on earth.

Neubra, Age 13 — Jacksonville, FL
Is there a mall in heaven?

They do not call it a mall, but there are many amazing, exciting places to go and get stuff and it is all free. Many people go shopping to get gifts for family members who will be coming to Heaven one day.

David, Age 40's — London, Canada
Are there guitars in heaven?

Yes, almost every kind of instrument ever created will be in Heaven. They even have bands and rock concerts as God LOVES all styles of music.

Alexis, Age 15 — Jacksonville, FL
Can I see my name in the lamb's book of life?

One day in Heaven, everyone will be able to see their names.

Lydia, Age 56 — Mississippi
Do they serve meat and fish in heaven?

Yes, they have all kinds of food, but it is made out of Light.

Judy, Age 55 - Golden, CO

Does the soul go to heaven? I know the spirit does.

You would not be you, if your soul (mind, will & emotions) didn't go to Heaven too.

ABOUT ONE QUEST INTERNATIONAL

A Florida Corporation

In obedience to the commission given by the Lord, One Quest International was formed as a for profit corporation to reveal Heaven to the people of the earth through published books, products, services and all forms of media. We are to also share about the Greater Glory (rather than the darkness) that is about to invade this earth with signs, wonders and the miraculous; which many call the 'former and latter rain' or the 'great awakening'. Whatever you choose to call it, it is Joel 2 manifesting in the earth through baptism in fire (the Love of God).

We are truly living in the most exciting time to be a Believer since the world was formed! One Quest International has a divine assignment to see and hear Heaven and reveal mysteries that have been hidden from the eyes of man!

The Word states in I Corinthians that, "Eye have not seen, nor ears heard, nor entered into the heart or mind of man what God has prepared for those who love Him, unless it be revealed by the Spirit of God" and as we enter into this divine season, God will be catching up many others to experience and share about His home, Heaven. Kat Kerr, President of One Quest, is one of those 'friends of God' who share with great passion, the wonders and beauty of the heavenly realm. Besides her best selling book series, Revealing Heaven, many future projects (using artists, designers, music & dance) are planned to carry out the purpose of their commission from the Lord to reach every age and people group with the TRUTH about Heaven!

CONTACT INFO: (904) 527-1943

Email: contactoqi@gmail.com

P. O. Box 550989

Jacksonville, FL 32255

www.revealingheaven.com

About the Author, Kat Kerr

➤┄◆➤╺◯╺◈┄◅

I accepted Jesus at age 5 and have had a close relationship with Him ever since. I have not led a perfect life, but quickly repented when I would sin. My Dad set a wonderful example for me and since I worked closely with him in his ministry of helping people for 18 years, my life has become an extension of his! I talk about my family a lot, because while growing up, they were all I had. They helped me to become who I am and I will always love them. 'Things' were not that important in our home and although we did not have much, we shared what we had.

If you are interested in my 'religious' credentials, here they are: I am a licensed minister (since 1981) although I do not use the title. Have operated in the prophetic (with a 'seer' anointing) for over 25 years. I trained and ministered under a proven prophet, Dr. Don Lynch, for several years. Through my home church, I was a member of our 'citywide' intercessory group and a member of the 'altar' ministry team. I have served in children's church, vacation bible school and headed up the hospitality team. Also, served in many positions at numerous conferences for various ministries and have been a part of our Victory ministry team for over 20 years.

The credentials which most impress the Lord are as follows: Honoring my parents at all times, not just as a child, but even now as an adult. Submitting to my wonderful husband for 29 years, even when I did not understand his decisions. Teaching the things of God to my three daughters; Kelly, Kimberly and Kasey, by LIVING the Word and not just speaking it. Giving extravagantly, even after losing everything during a season of my life and having to sleep on some else's floor. Developing a lifestyle of Abandoned Worship regardless of circumstances or situations evident in my life. Trusting Him like a child, unquestionably! Being thankful for everything He gives me, even the small things! Sharing what I have with others when they are in need. Setting aside hours every evening to worship and pray; and then waking every morning to greet The Father, my Lord Jesus and my best friend, Holy Spirit. A life lived for 'them' is my greatest credential!

I am so honored that God chose me for this assignment, even though I never asked. He has my permission to use me in any manner He chooses. You must live a 'surrendered' life to the will of the Father if you wish to pursue this type of intimate relationship. Prior to my experiences in Heaven, I had worked for twenty four years in key positions in the business world and now I am president of One Quest International Corp. which was founded for the purpose of revealing Heaven to the earth and providing 'Kingdom' finances'. Many projects are planned to take place in the near future to fulfill that vision.

About the Illustrator, Walter Reynolds

>-!-◆>-•Ⓞ-•<◆>-!-◄

The wonderful illustrations in this book are the combined effort of the Author who did all original sketches and Walter Reynolds, a gifted artist who received revelation from God and then brought them to life!

Walter is mostly self taught and has had no formal training beyond what he had in high school. Realizing he had a God given gift, he has spent many years perfecting it and then dedicated all his efforts to the bring Glory to the giver. Now the Holy Spirit expresses himself through Walter and what results is an artistic form of worship to Jesus. He is a humble person who feels honored to bring Heaven into the earthly realm so that all men may experience for themselves the world God has prepared for those who love him.

He is currently taking each of the illustrations and creating a finished work of art in brilliant color. Prints of these color illustrations will be made available on this website in the near future. His next project will be to illustrate the children's version of a book on Heaven that is being produced by One Quest International and authored by Jen Voorhees.

He is a freelance artist and is available for other projects. For info concerning Walter contact him through One Quest contact info.

STANDING WITH ISRAEL–
GOD'S CHOSEN

>─┤─◆┤──O──┤◆─┤─<

The following was written, at the request of the Father, by Paul Wilbur of Paul Wilbur Ministries.

Should Christians stand with the modern state of Israel? Is there a real connection between the Jewish community of today and the ancient people of the Bible? Are the promises of God through the prophets and the Psalms of David still valid today? Didn't the Church take the place of Israel in God's plan when the Jews rejected Christ and handed Him over to the Romans to be crucified?

The problem as I see it, is not a matter of truthful answers, but rather a matter of historically bad teaching and bias that has masked the truth with traditions of men that have made the word of God "of no effect."

"How have we done this" you might ask, "No one wants to be guilty of doing such a thing on purpose!" I am glad you asked, because it breaks ground for an honest look into the only answer we need, and they are contained within the pages of the Bible, God's word, perfect and eternal.

First of all, how we read the Bible, or better yet, how we understand the Bible is critical to our understanding of who the author is and what he has declared about Israel, covenant and the Jewish people. My dear friend John Bevere has been a Bible teacher for some twenty-five years, and on his last trip to Jacksonville he made a statement that will stick with me for the rest of my life! He said, and I paraphrase, "It is time for us to stop reading (the Bible) what we believe, and to start believing what we read!" Did you catch that? In other words, we are all guilty of reading the word of God through the rose colored glasses of the doctrines and traditions we have all been taught, rather than simply believing the words that we read on the page. We all feel inadequate at some point to completely and accurately understand and interpret certain passages of prophecy or allegory, so we turn to more learned men and women for help. The problem here is obvious; we each learn from one another, and sometimes we carry away 'truths' that are more tradition, conjecture or opinion than we were led to believe.

The sad thing to me as a Jewish believer is that so much of God's word could be so easily confused or misunderstood by more than 50% of the Church worldwide. All those promises that were made to Israel were contingent on how faithful she was as a nation? Wow, what a terrible standard and a burdensome stone to lay on anyone. How would you like all the promises of God to you to be contingent on how well the whole earth Church of America obeyed His commandments? No thank you!

So how should we understand the Bible on the subject of Israel and how should we respond to the Jewish people today? I have always believed that the Bible says what it means, and means what it says. Yes, there are many different kinds of Biblical language, prose, poetry, allegory, parables and the like, but most of it is pretty straightforward talk that is easily understood at face value. When God is speaking to Israel, He says so, and when He is speaking to the followers of Jesus, He makes it plain. It often takes several degrees and quite a few 'experts' to muddy it up beyond understanding!

So now that I have offended most of the educated world, or at least anyone with a few capital letters following their names, let's simply hear what the Bible has to say to and about Israel. When we know what the Creator of the Universe thinks about these things, it should make it a heck of a lot easier for us to make up our minds on which side of the debate we stand.

So let's hear from the author of the Bible, in His own words, what He thinks about Israel. (I have edited many of the following passages in order to conserve space without doing damage to the context. Any comments of mine will be in parenthesis)

Is. 41:9-10 O Israel, I have chosen you and not rejected you...do not fear for I am your God...I will strengthen you and help you...ALL who rage against you will surely be ashamed and disgraced...those who oppose you will perish. (You do not need to hold a doctorate of history degree to know that every nation that opposed Israel was put to shame.)

Jer.31:31 The time is coming, declares the Lord, when I will make a new covenant with the house of Israel and the house of Judah...For I will forgive their wickedness and will remember their sins no more... he who appoints the sun to shine by day, the moon and stars to shine by night, Adonai Sabbaoth is his name. Only if these decrees vanish from my sight will the descendants of Israel ever cease to be a nation before me.

Num.23:19 God is not a man that he should lie, or the son of man that he should repent and change his mind. Has he spoken and not performed it, or has he promised and not made it good?

Roms.11:1-22 I ask then, did God reject his people? BY NO MEANS! I am talking to you Gentiles...for if Israel's rejection is the reconciliation of the nations, what will Israel's acceptance be but life from the dead... (resurrection, the return of Yeshua, the Kingdom on earth). If the firstfruits is holy then the whole batch is holy; if the root is holy, so are the branches. Do not be arrogant, but be afraid. For if God did not spare the natural branches, he will not spare you either! (These are tough words, but the wise will humble themselves and take heed to what the Spirit of God is saying, even to the Church!)

Is.49:22-23 Behold I will lift up my hand in an oath to the nations, and they shall bring your sons in their arms, and your daughters shall be carried on their shoulders. Kings shall be your fathers and queens your nursing mothers; they shall bow before you with their faces to the earth and lick the dust of your feet. Then you will know that I am the Lord.

Joel 2:23-26 Be glad then you children of Zion, and rejoice in the Lord your God; and he will cause the rain to come down for you-the former rain and the latter rain...the threshing floors shall be full of wheat, and the vats shall overflow with new wine and oil. So I will restore to you the years that the locust has eaten...you shall eat and be satisfied, and praise the Name of the Lord your God; and my people Israel shall never be put to shame.

Obviously, these are just a small sampling of the hundreds of promises the God of Abraham, Isaac and Jacob has made to his people Israel. Isn't it just a little obvious to the casual observer when he uses the names of patriarchs of Israel for his own name?! He is identified many times in the scriptures in this way and never seems to mind. Even the life of Jesus parallels the life of Israel in many startling and amazing ways; born in Israel, went to Egypt, death of the innocents, and many more examples

Should Christians stand with Israel? I like to answer that question rather simply; does God love Israel?...then so should you!

Prophesies: given through Kat Kerr
From the Lord of Hosts,
"Do you really want more of me?

I n this season I will become very real to my people, but if there is too much self still in them, they will not even recognize me!

You must be willing to lay down your life in order to have my life. My plans for you are so much greater than you can imagine but you must trust me completely.

This has been a hard time, but I never left you even though it may have appeared to be so. Because you have remained faithful, I am about to consume you with my presence but you must be willing to receive me. Press into me. Press into me, so you do not miss me when I come!

There is great warfare commencing in the heavenlies because of the release that is about to take place.

Will you fight with them against me (by remaining full of yourself) or will you turn your whole heart towards me and yield it all (that you might be filled with me!) Worship me for who I am".

From the Father to His intercessors:

"My People, You breathe Me in when you praise Me; and when you testify of Me; you breathe Me out. Will you cleanse the air by praising Me and testifying of me or will you defile it by gossiping and complaining and backbiting? Do you want to walk in My light or will you walk in darkness and promote the enemy's kingdom?

Choose life and not death. Choose Me and not the spirit of the world. I have given you power through My Son. USE IT. Pray and Praise together. This region has a destiny that is vital to My purpose. Pray for it to come to pass. Pray for each other and then praise me for doing it. I love it when My people want My plan.

Angels have been released in this season to assist you. Your words spoken in faith release them to go forth- so release them and watch what I will do for you. My beloved people who have chosen to stand in the gap- a sweet aroma to Me and in My throne room. Great amounts of incense have been gathered into bowls. Watch what happens as I tip them over this region. It will never be the same.

I am a jealous God and I am jealous over you. Do not worry for the fear covering the earth- My Glory is much greater and you will SHINE with it! I LOVE YOU AND I HEAR YOU SAYS YOUR FATHER!"

PRODUCTS CATALOG
To order, Call (904) 527-1943
Or www.revealingheaven.com
(PRICES DO NOT INCLUDE SHIPPING)

BOOKS- $15.00

Revealing Heaven I

Revealing Heaven II, release Dec/2010

Revealing Heaven III, release 2011

Spanish Edition, Revealing Heaven I, release 2011

CHILDREN'S SERIES
(Price to be determined by publisher)

Adventures in Heaven (soon to be released)

AUDIO BOOKS - $20.00

Revealing Heaven I

Revealing Heaven II

DVD's- $15.00

Dancing with the Angels (Describes Heaven & the Heaven Invasion)

Living Worship (Worship in Heaven & worship on Earth) this DVD teaches the 'angel' dance

Ancient Paths (where we lived in Heaven before coming to Earth)

Heaven Celebrates (Heavens view of death)

CD's SINGLE DISC- $5.00

Heaven Rocks (For Youth age 10 to 25 or the Young at Heart)

Throne Room Declarations (God speaking to our Government & declaring what He is about to do to His people)

Beyond the Veil (What happens when someone dies, the beauty of Heaven)

Ancient Paths (Tells where we lived in Heaven before coming to earth & describes the Heart of the Father)

CD DOUBLE SET- $10.00

Celestial Realm (hours of info about places in Heaven)

Dancing with the Angels (see DVD above for info)

Daddy's Girls (How the Father spoils His daughters in Heaven - shopping spree, He give us Bling, our children living in Heaven)

CD SERIES 8 DISC SET- $35.00

Heaven Invasion: Taped in Canada - a four part series I, II, III, IV giving in-depth information about Heaven and Heaven coming to earth

CD SERIES 6 DISC SET- $ 25.00

Divine Encounter: Taped in Mississippi, a three part series I, II, III

More info about Heaven and about the spirit realm around us, also how satan operates in our lives)

CD SERIES 3 DISC SET - $12.00

WILD WEST HEAVEN FEST – Colorado Women's Conference

Sat Morning and Saturday Afternoon for women only – POWERFUL

CD SERIES 8 DISC SET $35.00 (purchased separately $10.00)

COLORADO HEAVEN EXPLOSION

Saturday Evening: Life with Your Mom, Wife or Daughter has a lot of humor

Sunday: Amazing revelations

Monday: Youth meeting, UNSPOKEN (radical in EVERY way)

Tuesday: Becoming the Violent that TAKE IT by force

CDS IN ANY SERIES MAY BE PURCHASED INDIVIDUALLY

ILLUSTRATIONS FROM VOLUME I & II

8 1/2 x 11 - $4.00 each

11 x 17 - $12.00 each

"EYES OF ETERNITY" COVER ARTWORK

From VOL I (Teal) or VOL II (Sapphire Blue):

11 x 17- $20.00

16 x 20- $25.00

20 x 24- $35.00

PHOTOS OF ANGELS in the SKY

FIRE ANGEL - a 200 ft angel carrying fire into Florida

BREATH OF GOD - face of the Angel of the Lord (in clouds) blowing breath of God

THE GUARDIAN - face of an Angel looking down from Heaven

8 1/2 x 11 - $5.00 each

11 x 17 - $15.00 each

SUGGESTED READING:

Revealing Heaven I
Author: Kat Kerr

Kisses from Heaven release date 2011
Author: Melodie Nobles (Maurissa's Mother)

The Final Quest
Author: Rick Joyner

The Heaven's Opened
Author: Anna Rountree

The Blood and The Glory
Author: Billye Brim

The Twelve Stones of Revelation
Author: Mary Trask

NOTES

PRAYER LIST

PRAYER LIST